The Atomic Bomb
That Exploded—
8,000 Years Ago!

In Pakistan, in what used to be the Indus Valley of India, there are ruins of several ancient cities that are credited with having contained, within their immense areas, populations of well over a million each. . . . The largest are now called Mohenjo-Daro and Harappa, although we have no idea what their names were when they flourished. . . . Apparently both of these cities were destroyed suddenly; excavations down to the street level have revealed scattered skeletons, as if doom had come so swiftly that the inhabitants did not have time to get to their houses. These skeletons, after thousands of years, are still among the most radioactive that have ever been found, on a par with those of Hiroshima and Nagasaki.

D0816183

Charles Berlitz

DOOMSDAY 1999 A.D.

with collaboration, maps and drawings by J. Manson Valentine

PUBLISHED BY POCKET BOOKS NEW YORK

POCKET BOOKS, a Simon & Schuster division of
GULF & WESTERN CORPORATION
1230 Avenue of the Americas, New York, N.Y. 10020

To the world of the future—
if there is one . . .

Contents

DOOMSDAY
1999 A.D.

1

Doomsday
1999 A.D.

The end of the world, whether by flood, fire, freezing, cosmic collision or other catastrophic manifestations, has always had a grim fascination for prophets of doom and also for the general population. The makers of such predictions are of several varieties. They are religious prophets of warning, mystic prophets—basically a variant of the former—and seers who seem to dream inadvertently of future events without living to see their prophecies fulfilled. Then there are the scientific interpreters of trends and likely possibilities of doom who frequently indicate, supported by the evidence of astronomy, geology, meteorology, and even economics, an even more complete destruction than many of the prophetic visions from the past.

The scientific prophets of today foresee the pillaging and eventual destruction of the earth's potential through uncontrolled industrialization; general famine resulting from overpopulation and food distribution breakdown; disastrous climatic variation and flooding through the hothouse effect of excessive carbon dioxide in the upper atmospheric layers; and the poisoning of the oceans and the destruction of the sea's ability to renew life. These threats to survival are generally conceded to become acute toward the end of the second millennium of our era—the year 2000 A.D.

11

There are, understandably, a great number of thoughtful people in the general population who fatalistically expect a possible Doomsday from the results of thermonuclear warfare, with the added possibility of a self-generating chain reaction which, in the opinion of some theoreticians, might possibly turn the earth into a temporary though short-lived sun. These ever present eventualities, while they may or may not cause the world to end, have nevertheless contributed liberally to the increasing neurosis of human beings. This neurosis may explain the turning of a basically moralistic society into a hedonistic (and increasingly violent) one, acceptable for many individuals but not valid in the long run as the example of the decay and disappearance of the Roman world empire can brilliantly attest.

As nation after nation develops its own nuclear warfare capabilities in a sort of international contest of self-esteem it is evident that within the next fifteen to twenty years all industrial or developed countries, as well as all developing countries which are striving and being helped to become developed as soon as possible, will doubtless have their own nuclear weapons. And with the testing of such weapons the poisoning of the planet will be hastened, even if war does not come.

And, as if potential man-made dooms were not enough, there is an increasing possibility that the earth, as it approaches the second millennium of our era, may experience a wandering of its magnetic poles so far away from its rotational poles (the southern magnetic pole is even now rushing with increased velocity into the Indian Ocean) that it could cause a shifting of the poles and a reversal of the magnetic fields of the earth with catastrophic consequences. In addition, the tides of the second, inner layer of the earth's crust, the magma of the asthenosphere, may be affected in 1982 when the greater planets—Jupiter, Saturn, Uranus, Neptune and our own sun and moon come into direct alignment with the earth. It is now considered by certain astronomers that this alignment of the planets may cause the magma layer to pile up within the crust and change the balance of the world, causing a "wobble" which would mean that the earth would undergo major geological changes. These changes would mean huge tidal waves, tempests with wind speeds of hundreds of miles per hour, earthquakes of intensity far beyond the Richter scale, the sinking of islands, coastal areas, and low-lying inland areas and the rising to above sea level of sections of the ocean floor. Those of us who witnessed such manifestations would in effect feel that the end of our world had come, a feeling doubtless shared by many in the distant past when the Great Flood (of which catastrophe the deluge may have been only one aspect) swept over the world, and great inhabited islands sank into the Atlantic and other seas.

Although 1982, the year in which these planets will be aligned, is still a year away, some of these changes may have already started. The earth's weather, either caused by sunspots or the beginning of a change in the magnetic field, has become increasingly erratic and intense. The great Sahel drought famine in Africa has been the worst in hundreds of years; the rising and falling of water levels and coastlines in different parts of the world; the melting of the Arctic ice cap and the rapid building of ice in the Antarctic continent; and the increase in the number and rating on the Richter scale of earthquakes within the last few years in Alaska, Iran, Turkey, China, Peru, and Morocco, with impressive seismic occurrences expected almost momentarily along the San Andreas fault of California, are impressive warnings for those who will heed them. Not only the number but also the *intensity* of earthquakes seems to be increasing throughout the world in a sort of geometric progression, even as seismologists perfect new methods to foretell them. (So far seismologists have yet to improve on earthquake detection methods apparently inherent in animals: when Russian bears leave their Siberian forests in a hurry observers know from experience that an earthquake is sure to follow.)

There may also be more danger from space itself than an occasional falling skylab or space station. The earth is pitted with enormous craters caused by meteorite impact, some of them on the sea bottom, other huge ones covered over or partly obscured by growth or settlements, while others are strikingly evident, such as the meteorite crater in Arizona. Other "bombs" from outer space have left huge lakes in Canada like Clearwater Lake, a whole depressed area in Central Europe, the Ries Kessel crater, and, it has been theorized, a crater which filled with water to become Hudson Bay. There is also a circular area of the western Atlantic south of Bermuda which may have received a tremendous cosmic bolide tentatively dated at the alleged time of the disappearance of lost Atlantis. While the earth's atmosphere has provided a stronger shield against these voyagers from space than that of the moon or Mars, a certain amount have slipped past Earth's protective guard to leave great scars, and perhaps when big enough, to cause the shaking of the earth upon its axis.

Coincidentally with the possible catastrophe by 2,000, there exists a planetoid, Toro, some five kilometers in diameter, which orbits between Earth and Venus, making a loop once in every five orbits. While there is no danger to the earth from Toro in its present orbit, a gravitational pull occasioned by the lining up of several planets and the sun might capture Toro within the earth's field of gravity, a situation having results perhaps similar to those caused by strikings of the earth by comets, planetoids, or enormous meteors in the past. Such an alignment of earth, the sun, and the greater planets will take place in 1982.

A curious and somewhat disquieting coincidence is becoming increasingly evident as the twentieth century or second millennium draws to a close. This coincidence, rooted in both the distant and the recent past, ties in the prophecies of hundreds and even thousands of years ago with the cosmic theories and scientific realities of the present. Prophecies of the world's end by fire, ice, water, or explosion, although made in different ages and by different cultures during the past 6,000 years, seem to agree that the age of doom is fairly close at hand, that is, toward the end of our second millennium by whatever calendar or zodiacal calculation used by the prophets.

Some of the most fearful prophecies from the past are alarmingly close in content and in time location to today's pessimistic scientific forecasts, although the prophets of other centuries, insofar as we know, had no access other than their imagination to scientific developments in what to them was the distant (but not unforeseeable) future.

There existed, however, even in antiquity the great time clock in the night sky, which we still share with our ancestors. This is the zodiac, a great turning wheel of twelve constellations making a complete circle every 25,920 years but with each of its twelve constellations in order having ascendancy over the skies of earth approximately every 2,160 years. Observed and calculated even before the development of writing (which may itself have been a result of zodiacal influence) this great celestial cosmic calendar signified certain portents to our most distant ancestors who, like many of their descendants, detected its influence in their lives.

According to zodiacal tradition the ascendency of each new sign every 2,000-odd years is accompanied by catastrophic or otherwise crucial events on the earth. At the changeover of the Leo to Cancer cycles the sinking of the great Atlantic islands traditionally took place; the Cancer to Gemini change coincided with the presumed striking of the earth by a comet or the catastrophic arrival of Venus; the appearance of Taurus after Gemini marked the beginning or recommencement of new civilizations in the ancient East; Taurus to Aries brought a new series of floods and catastrophes; while the Aries to Pisces change coincided with the rise and spread of Christianity (it is of particular interest that early Christianity was first identified by the sign of the fish, an early symbol adopted even before the cross).

As we pass the cosmic border from Pisces to Aquarius our own tumultuous age has been foreseen as one of materialistic degeneration and maximum destruction especially at its beginning, which is now. This general tradition has perhaps been colored by many of the world's ancient as well as by fairly recent prophets.

Nostradamus, the sixteenth-century French prophet (of Jewish descent), abandoned his usually vague and veiled references for a precise date when he stated:

> The year 1999, month seven,
> From the sky shall come a great king of terror . . .

Those of us still alive in 1999 will be able to judge the perceptiveness of Nostradamus' most precisely dated prophecy.

Edgar Cayce, perhaps the most famous of modern prophets, because of his remarkable record of verification, has sketched, in his transcribed dreams, a time of imminent future catastrophe for a large part of the earth; the sliding of Japan into the Pacific Ocean, earthquakes which will destroy California, the permanent inundation of coastal cities throughout the world and the reappearance of new lands (and ancient continents) thrust up from the ocean floor. While predicated within our present time frame, the start of this chain of catastrophic events will be recognized by the renewed volcanic activity of Mount Etna—which has already started.

Religious prophecies of a final end to the world or civilization are frequently predicated on other events which will signal their occurrence. The ancient Jewish prophets foretold that Armageddon would occur after a Jewish state had been reestablished. Speaking from several thousands of years ago their voices seem to ring with the accent of today's political commentators as they prophesy in the Old Testament that the final battle and the final coming of the Messiah will occur *within a generation* after the reestablishment of the Jews in their ancient homeland.

The final war of general annihilation according to the Biblical prophets will be occasioned by attacks from peoples living to the north and south of Israel, which will be opposed by Israel and its allies. While we do not know the actual date these prophecies were made they antedate the New Testament by at least a thousand years and perhaps thousands of years.

From other of the world's religions or cosmic theogonies come indications of doom whose signals have taken place within our own "end of Pisces" time frame. Tibetan Buddhist prophecies that Tibetan Buddhism would end after the thirteenth Dalai Lama would be dethroned (he has been) and the general Buddhist prophecy that Buddhism would last for 2,500 years, a period now ending, both agree that the final world period will be at hand for the coming of the future Buddha, Maitreya.

An unexpected prophetic development occurred in the case of the Islamic prophecy that Islam would last until man set foot on the moon, a hyperbole signifying an indefinite period but which caused consternation in conservative Islamic circles when Armstrong and Aldrin finally did so. Islamic traditionalists, however, have argued that the astronauts did not land on the real moon—"the lamp of the night"—but on some other heavenly body. Therefore the prophecy has not been fulfilled and, in any case, Islam seems to be affirmatively flourishing.

The pyramid prophecies as interpreted by psychic pyramidologists indicate in the turns and measurements of the inner galleries of the Great Pyramid at Gizeh, Egypt, the end of the world in the year 2001 of our era. The decline is said to have started in 1965, the latter date a finding with which many economists will doubtless agree. Also, the ancient Aztec age cycles as well as the probably connected Hopi cyclic age endings both predict an end to the world at the end of the present period—the sun of fire. Hindu tradition, as expressed in the ancient Puranas, also foretells a possible annihilation of the human race at the end of the fourth or kali yuga (and remember that Kali is the goddess of destruction), the present age now drawing to a close.

Whatever may be one's scientific theories, cosmological traditions, or religious beliefs, it is nevertheless an unusual coincidence that cataclysmic doom seems to be generally expected by approximately the year 2000 A.D. Other cultures, while guarding their own religious counts of time, as in the case of the Chinese, Arabs, Jews, and others, have generally accepted the western system of counting years because of the easier common calculations. There seems, nevertheless, to exist a common zodiacal thread—the change of "hour" or era of the dominant constellation of our shared cosmic clock every 2,160 years. This may have influenced the inception of Christianity itself or, conversely, been signaled by it.

It is also perhaps to be expected that humanity may consider that every thousand-year period will be accompanied by earth-shaking events. The very word millennium, originally simply a count of one thousand years, has taken on a meaning alternately of destruction, death, redemption, retribution, and—hope.

Toward the arrival of the last millennium—December 31, 999 A.D.—so many people in the Christian lands of that time actually thought that the world was coming to an end that they proceeded to act in an unaccustomed fashion. In their dealings with each other they became so brotherly, so charitable, so filled with self-abnegation and love for their neighbor that the true millennium, however briefly, seemed to be at hand.

It is, of course, regrettable that generally only in moments of impending doom do whole populations tend to forget their own immediate and selfish interests and join together in a brief brotherhood of mutual help and kindness. This is how it was during the month of December 999 A.D.

2

Doomsday—
December 31st,
999 A.D.

Legend, prophecy, and general expectation of the millennium had led the Christian world to anticipate that at midnight, December 31st, 999 A.D. the world would come to an end. The form of the world's end varied somewhat according to locality and individual belief; in the Germanic and Slavic lands of the north it would end in fire, in the Mediterranean countries a great blast from Gabriel's trumpet would summon the dead from their graves to share a last judgment with all those who had not yet died. Christ would return to earth and would lead true believers to Paradise.

As the year 999 neared its end a sort of mass hysteria took hold of Europe. All forms of activity became affected by the specter of impending doom. Even though "the just" should have been expected to look forward to a more immediate entrance into Paradise than previously supposed, no one could be sure how "just" he might be considered at the Last Judgment and therefore a considerable extra effort was assuredly called for.

Men forgave each other their debts, husbands and wives confessed suspected and unsuspected infidelities to each other and were mutually forgiven, poachers proclaimed their unlawful poachings to the lords of manors and then, although permitted by the nobles to continue their punishable actions, did not do so, demanding only forgiveness.

As the year rolled on toward its end, commerce between towns and cities was largely interrupted; dwellings were neglected and let fall into ruin; what was the use of storing up wealth if it might be held against you in the Final Judgment, as the Biblical parable of the rich man and the "eye of the needle" clearly proclaimed? Beggars were liberally fed by the more fortunate, those convicted of crimes were released from prison although many wanted to remain in prison, crying that they wished to expiate their sins before the end. In direct obedience to the gospel, the rich gave away their splendid garments to the needy: "If a man asks you for your coat—give him your cloak also." Others, however, kept their best garments at hand so that they might be as well dressed as possible when called upon to meet their Maker. The churches, the gates of monasteries and convents, and the great cathedrals were constantly besieged by crowds demanding confession and absolution. Masses of general absolution, at a time when Christianity was still a united faith, were conducted day and night with crowds of people unable to enter standing outside the great doors.

It is difficult for urban dwellers of the present day to appreciate the towering and awe-inspiring presence of the churches and cathedrals of the Middle Ages. They dwarfed other buildings in the towns and cities and were often visible from far out in the countryside as well. Besides serving as places of worship, they were beacons, refuges, centers of assembly and charity, and burial places for kings and queens, prelates and nobles. The sight of these awesome constructions with spires reaching up to the heavens, and inside vaults suggesting the celestial halls of the hereafter, were a constant reminder of one's faith and fate. And consequently, toward the end of the year 999 they served as a continuing warning to the dwellers in the castles and manors, merchants in the town, or laborers in the fields, of the common fate they could expect at the stroke of midnight on the last day of that fateful year.

Pilgrims flocked to Jerusalem (this was before the restrictive measures from the Moslem Turks that brought on the Crusades) from points all over Europe. Knights, burghers of the towns, and even serfs, all traveling together, many with their wives and children, journeyed eastward in great bands. Class differences were forgotten in an outpouring of Christian brotherhood. As they marched some whipped themselves in punishment for past sins while others sang hymns and psalms. As they walked they constantly turned their eyes toward the sky. In the twilight and the night sky the penitents saw portents that reaffirmed what they believed to be approaching doom. They saw flaming swords and arrows traversing the heavens, much as watchers of a later day expecting to see UFOs often do see them.

When December arrived mass psychosis and fanaticism appeared as well, springing from the dark side of human nature. Groups of flagellants roamed through the countryside, scourging each other and congregating in the market places of towns where they left trails of blood leading up to the doors of the churches. In some areas mobs formed, shouting for and often obtaining the death of rich merchants, usurers, and suspected magicians, so that after the execution of these unpopular burghers the inhabitants of a given locality might report to the Angel of Judgment that the immediate area was free of the ungodly. There was a wave of suicides as people sought to punish themselves in advance of Doomsday or simply could not stand the pressure of waiting for Judgment Day.

Christmas passed—perhaps the last Christmas the world would ever know—with an outpouring of piety and love. Families felt renewed bonds of love, and lovers contrived to stay constantly together in the final hours. (The wave of marriages noted in the earlier part of the year had subsided, perhaps in realization of the Biblical admonition that there is "no marriage or giving in marriage in Heaven.") After Christmas what we, in a more cynical and less credulous age, would call "countdown" began in earnest.

Farm animals were freed as their owners prepared for death and final judgment. Some of the animals wandered over the countryside but others stayed close to their stables. Horses freed within the towns trotted hither and yon until they came to the town gates. Here sentries allowed them to pass and they left the towns for the open country and freedom. Cows waiting to be milked mooed plaintively but the routine of farm life had vanished temporarily as prayers replaced work in the final days of the year. Food shops and bakeries gave away their goods and refused the coins that were pressed upon them. In the warmer lands of Italy, Spain, and Southern France the infirm and the dying in hospitals and convents begged to be carried out into the open so they could personally see Christ as He descended from the skies.

As the night of December 31 approached the general frenzy reached new heights. In Rome the immense Basilica of St. Peter's was crowded for the midnight mass which in the belief of many might be the last mass they would ever attend on earth. A dramatic account of this incident described by a modern historian, Frederick H. Martens, in *The Story of Human Life* furnishes a striking example of what happened that night in cathedrals and churches throughout Europe:

> . . . Pope Sylvester II stood before the high altar. The church was overcrowded, all in it lay on their knees. The silence was so great that the rustling of the Pope's white sleeves as he moved about the altar could be heard. And there was still another sound. It was a

sound that seemed to measure out the *last minutes of
the earth's thousand years of existence since the coming of Christ!* It echoed in the ears of those present as
the pulse-beat does in the ears of a man with a fever,
and its beat was loud and regular and never stopped.
For the door of the church sacristy stood open, and
what the audience heard was the regular, uninterrupted
tick, tick, tock of the great clock which hung within,
one tick for every passing second.

The Pope was a man of iron will-power, calm and
collected. He had probably left the sacristy door open
purposely, in order to secure the greatest amount of
effect at this great moment. Though his face was pale as
death with excitement, he did not move nor did his
hands tremble.

The midnight mass had been said, and a deathly
silence fell. The audience waited . . . Pope Sylvester
said not a word. He seemed lost in prayer, his hands
raised to the sky. The clock kept on ticking. A long sigh
came from the people, but nothing happened. Like
children afraid of the dark, all those in the church lay
with their faces to the ground, and did not venture to
look up. The sweat of terror ran from many an icy
brow, and knees and feet which had fallen asleep lost
all feeling.

Then, suddenly—the clock stopped ticking!

Among the congregation the beginning of a scream of
terror began to form in many a throat. And, stricken
dead by fear, several bodies dropped heavily on the
stone floor.

Then the clock began to strike. It struck one, two,
three, four . . . It struck twelve. . . . The twelfth stroke
echoed out, and a deathly silence still reigned!

Then it was that Pope Sylvester turned around, and
with the proud smile of a victor stretched out his hands
in blessing over the heads of those who filled the
church. And at the same moment all the bells in the
tower began to peal out a glad and jubilant chime, and
from the organ-loft sounded a chorus of joyous voices,

young and older, a little uncertain at first, perhaps, but growing clearer and firmer moment by moment. They sang the *Te Deum Laudamus*—"Thee, God, we praise!"

The whole congregation united their voices with those of the choir. Yet it was some time before cramped backs could be straightened out, and before people recovered from the dreadful sight offered by those who had died of fright. When the *Te Deum* had been sung, men and women fell in each other's arms, laughing and crying and exchanging the kiss of peace. Thus ended the thousandth year after the birth of Christ!

It is to be expected that not long after the moment of suspense passed, life resumed its normal medieval rhythm, the merchants ceased giving away their goods, the owners or others captured the wandering cows and sheep and put the horses back to work, and whatever criminals could be located were put back into prison after their brief respite. One supposes also that the monies and goods given away by the rich were not returned, unless in understandably rare cases, when those so gifted could be found. Nevertheless, the common traumatic experience was a good exercise, for a short time, in love and forgiveness toward one's neighbor—the basic teaching of Christianity.

Other events since then have been characterized as indications of the coming doom of mankind, at least as far as Europe was concerned. These included the Black Death, racial memories of which are still with us. The number of victims has been calculated to be one third of the population of Europe in the thirteenth century—that is, thirty to thirty-five million persons—dying in such conditions of suffering that it seemed to survivors, bemused by scenes of horror and the dancing madness of wandering crowds, that the true end of the world was at hand.

Other predicted dooms, such as the invasion of Europe by the Mongols and later by the Turks, while final enough for the Europeans who were slain, were more localized and often temporary in scope. The Europeans, recovering from these dooms of the Middle Ages, soon became a world-ending force of their own after the discovery of the Americas, when they fell upon the native population of the New World almost annihilating them with guns, swords, and disease.

None of these events, however, has seriously affected the constant proliferation of mankind. Nations disappear and new ones emerge, new peoples and classes develop, patterns of life and the means of supporting life change, but humanity, despite new wars, increasing starvation, and new diseases, has constantly increased. While there has been no "end of the world" generally expected since our scientific techniques have been perfected within the last one hundred years, it is rather ironic that this same expertise may be the cause and also the announcer of an imminent future doom more real than the collectively imagined one of *almost* one thousand years ago.

3

Ancient Prophecies:
The World Ends
by 2000 A.D.

Throughout the world of today, already beset by a multitude of other worries, there is growing an increasing nervousness about a cosmic event that will occur in 1982. The preview of these effects may already have begun. This occurrence will mark, by a coincidence in their orbits, a concentration of most of the planets in our solar system on the side of the sun opposite the earth. This will occur around Christmas time 1982 and, it is theorized, the pull of the planets on the sun will cause sunspots, flares, and possibly resultant earthquakes around the world and also, through the tidal effects exercised on the inner core of the earth, cause enormous earthquakes especially at the boundaries of the slowly moving tectonic plates on which the land masses and the oceans ride. These temblors, occurring along fault lines, such as that of San Andreas, may be of much higher intensity than those of the past and might initiate a self-propagating earthquake era, with disastrous results for civilization. As earthquakes have been increasing in frequency and intensity during the last decade, some scientists as well as psychic observers have suggested that the approaching global catastrophe has already started and that the great earthquakes of the sixties and seventies in Peru, China, Alaska, Mexico, Turkey, and Iran are merely the before shocks of greater seismic catastrophes to come.

According to British astronomers John Gribbin and Stephen H. Plagemann *(The Jupiter Effect:* 1974), an even more dangerous condition will exist in May, 2000 A.D. for those of us who are here to observe it. At this time Mercury, Mars, and Earth will be in direct allineation with the huge planets Saturn and Jupiter as well as with Pluto and the earth's moon. Venus will also be close to Mercury in this cosmic line-up. The effect of powerful earthquakes brought about by this positioning might be strong enough to disturb the earth's rotation, causing it to wobble on its axis and perhaps to bring about a magnetic reversal of its poles.

But this "worst case" situation, which is now being commented on with increasing frequency by present-day astronomers, geologists, and oceanographers was also noted and commented on by Berossus, a Babylonian astrologer-historian who lived more than 2,300 years ago. One wonders through what telescopic equipment and what lost techniques Berossus and the Babylonian magicians (then a word for astronomers) arrived at their calculations. The Roman poet, Seneca, related some 300 years later what Berossus originally caused to be inscribed in wedge-shaped cuneiform syllables pressed into wet clay tablets:

> . . . these events take place according to the course of the stars; and affirm it so positively, as to assign the time for the Conflagration and the Deluge. He maintains that all terrestrial things will be consumed when the planets, which now are traversing their different courses, shall all coincide in the sign of Cancer, and be so placed that a straight line could pass directly through all their orbs. But the inundation will take place when the same conjunction of the planets shall occur in

Capricorn. The first in the summer, the last in the winter of the year . . .

Berossus, in speaking of "the year" was referring to the sidereal year, the precession of the equinoxes, which takes 25,827 of our years. (This figure is the time it takes the earth's polar axis, which changes in space from day to day, to return to its original position in space in relation to the zodiacal band. The twelve constellations of the zodiacal band as they succeed each other in the night sky have formed a convenient cosmic clock for earth observers for many thousands of years.)

Was Berossus making a prophecy or merely an educated guess several millennia in advance of his time, based on many millennia of observation and research before his own era? The astronomical observations of distant antiquity, generally connected with prophecy, were often included in legends of the gods or disguised as a code, perhaps to restrict the information to the priestly caste. The extent of the sidereal year can be recognized in the sum of the crossed diagonals of the Great Pyramid at Gizeh which give a total of 25,826.6 pyramidal inches. How did Berossus know about, or the Fourth dynasty of Egypt measure the sidereal year? And this is only one example of cosmic information contained in the Great Pyramid.

While archaeologists generally accept the Pharaoh Cheops (Khufu) of the IV dynasty as the builder of the Great Pyramid, this is questioned by a tradition held by the Copts, the purest descendants of the ancient Egyptian stock. This tradition declares that the Great Pyramid was there for many centuries *before* Khufu, thereby inferring that Khufu may have repaired it only and then have taken credit for its construction (a maneuver not unknown to the rulers of Egypt who often "erased" their predecessors' names from monuments and substituted their own).

According to a history of ancient Egypt written by

Masoudi, a medieval Coptic historian, the two greatest pyramids (those of Cheops and Chephren) were built by Surid, one of the Kings of Egypt *before* the flood, who built them as a result of a prophetic dream wherein "the sky came down and the stars fell upon the earth." His interpreters of dreams, when queried, predicted that "a great flood would come accompanied by a fire from the constellation Leo, which would burn up the world. King Surid thereupon ordered the two pyramids to be built and to be recorded through their walls all the secret sciences together with knowledge of the stars as well as all they knew of mathematics and geometry, so that they would be a witness for those who would come after them."

Some of the other measurements and calculations yield surprising results, almost as if the Great Pyramid, as has been mentioned by Egyptian Coptic writers in the intervening centuries, is not a tomb but a compendium of mathematical and astronomical knowledge. For example:

1. Base perimeter divided by twice the height = 3.1416.*
2. Fifty pyramidal inches = 1 ten millionth of the earth's polar axis.**
3. Base perimeter = 356,240 pyramidal inches (or number of days in year).
4. Height × 1,000,000,000 = approximate distance of earth to sun at autumnal equinox.
5. Weight of pyramid × 1 trillion = approximate weight of the earth.
6. Base perimeter × 2 = 1 minute of a degree at the Equator.

---

* The modern value of Pi. Archimedes, the famous Greek mathematician, who lived thousands of years later, never got closer than 3.1428.

** Some among the ancient Egyptians must have had access to information indicating the true size and weight of the earth. The shape was well known to them and the concept of a round earth in space was taught to young students at the priestly schools.

Because of the scientific information still being discovered within the Great Pyramid, a belief has grown among psychics that there must be a message of prophecy indicated by measurements of the interior passageways calculated by pyramidal inches. Measurements have revealed a series of breaks and variations built into the twists, turns, and protuberances of the galleries and inner chambers which are considered as indicative of important events in the past, the present, and the future. Believers in these prophecies have included at least one well known astronomer, Charles Piazzi Smyth, once the Astronomer Royal of Scotland. These predictions in stone are believed by many pyramidologists to have begun on a date equivalent to September 22, 4000 B.C., and will end on September 17, 2001 A.D., the end of the sixth millennium.

While remembering that this is an interpretive prophecy, mainly after the fact, it is still intriguing to observe that certain modern events appear to have been indicated in advance, that is, *since* the time the key was thought to have been discovered in the early part of the twentieth century—the gallery measurements apparently indicated critical events which would occur at dates corresponding to World War I, the Armistice, World War II, the Atomic Age, and crucial events of the fifties and seventies. But the measurements—and history itself—seem to break off in 2001.

A calculation by Heraclitus of Ephesus, a Greek philosopher of the Ionian school, can be interpreted as a forecast of the next world catastrophe. Ancient Greek cosmic outlook was influenced by a theory held by Plato and other philosophers that there were and would be periodic destructions of the earth by fire and flood. Heraclitus, who was not influenced by Plato's account of the destruction of Atlantis, since he predated him, calculated that the world would be destroyed *again* in 10,800 years, counting from the last time it suffered almost total destruction. If we take

Heraclitus' time span of recurring catastrophes and calculate it from a date in Plato's account of the sinking of Atlantis (9,000 years before *his* time) we obtain a date for the next catastrophe fairly close to the end of the second millennium. This theory was proposed centuries before our present year count began. It is one more instance of a correlation in time of ancient predictions of catastrophes, kept alive in various world traditions throughout the centuries.

Scientific expertise and cosmic information interpreted through legends mixed with prophecy sometimes occur in remote corners of the world far removed from the advanced cultures of Egypt, Greece, and Mesopotamia.

The Hopi, a small Amerindian tribe of very ancient traditions, apparently knew that the earth turned on its axis. In a Hopi legend the axis of the earth was guarded by a pair of cosmic giants who, when they left their positions, caused the earth to falter in its spin, resulting in the end of a world and the start of a new era, eventually to be followed by still another. The beginning of the end of the present or Fourth World is considered by the Hopi to have already started and will be consummated after the appearance of a now invisible star, rushing toward Earth from space. Strangely, the Hopi concept of catastrophe caused by the earth faltering on its axis is a preoccupation among certain scientists of today and yesterday who, attributing the future cause to overloading of ice on the poles, shifting of the inner magma tides of the earth, a series of earthquakes and volcanic eruptions, or a cosmic collision or near collision, foresee basically the same results as the Hopi prophetic visions—the world's end in earthquake and fire.

Toltec-Aztec world-ending concepts also prophesied that the present world or sun would end within the present era by earthquakes, a cataclysmic denouement shared by Berossus of Babylon, ancient prophets, medieval seers, and a number of modern astronomers and psychics.

Within the Judeo-Christian religious tradition there exist in the Bible, as expressed by some of the Old Testament prophets, predictions in which although the years are not mentioned, certain conditions are specified which seem to locate the end of the present world within our own time period, very close to now, the final days being identified as the time soon after the Jews have been established once more in their own land. At this time, as written in Zechariah 14, the Lord declares: ". . . I will gather all nations against Jerusalem to battle . . ." These prophecies are also contained within Ezekiel chapters 36, 37, 38; in Daniel, 11, 12; Joel 2 and 3; and Isaiah 23 and 24.

In the Book of Ezekiel we find a specific reference in the Lord's prophecy to Ezekiel recalling the scattering of Israel "among the heathen" in the past. But the Lord promises that He will "gather you out of all countries and will bring you into your own land. . ." and that ". . . the wastes shall be builded . . . and the desolate land shall be tilled . . ." and ". . . the waste cities shall be filled with flocks of men . . . I will make them one nation in the land upon the mountain of Israel."

However, further along in Ezekiel's prophecy, we find that a great invasion shall come from "Gog" in the north and a great war will ensue when "everyman's hand will be against his brother." This prophecy continues with a promise of divine intervention—"with pestilence and with blood . . . and I will rain upon him, and upon his bands . . . an overflowing rain and great hailstones, fire, and brimstone . . . and I shall send a fire on Magog . . ." and "seven months shall the house of Israel be burying them."

These predictions have been interpreted by many Biblical students as a direct reference to the final battle of Armageddon, when Jerusalem will be attacked by many nations and the next millenium will be at hand. As this attack and threat of attack is located within the present century, if we link it to the prophesied return of the Jews to Israel, we have the feeling that Biblical prophecy is being corroborated by events in the daily press.

Hal Lindsey, author and theological student *(The Late Great Planet Earth:* 1970) even suggests a battle plan, based on Daniel's prophecies such as, *"at the time of the end* (italics added) the king of the south shall push at him (Israel) and the king of the north shall come against him like a whirlwind . . . with chariots, with horsemen, and with many ships . . ."* A somewhat free interpretation of the above and the ensuing verses indicates to the author a Russian amphibious assault to the south of Israel, to coincide with an invasion from the northern flank to push down through Israel north to south before the final battle is joined at Armageddon. After this conflict the Day of Judgment will come: ". . . many of them that sleep in the dust of the earth shall awake, some to everlasting life and some to shame and contempt."

The prophecies in Joel deal with destruction before a future Day of Judgment as they describe: ". . . wonders in the heavens and in the earth, blood and fire, and pillars of smoke—the sun shall be turned into darkness and the moon into blood, before the great and the terrible day of the Lord come." And in Isaiah, we also hear rumblings of a future doom, one with cosmic overtones: ". . . the windows from on high are opened, and the foundations of the earth do shake . . . the earth is utterly broken down . . . The earth shall reel to and fro like a drunkard . . . it shall fall and not rise again. . . . The Lord maketh the earth empty . . . and turneth it upside down . . ."

In the New Testament the mystical and frequently obscure Book of Revelation of St. John of Patmos contains vivid descriptions of the catastrophes which will occur during the approaching period of the Apocalypse and the Final Judgment and refers to a final battle, the greatest of earth's history. This will be the Battle of Armageddon (Meggido, on the map) in which will contend an attacking army of 200,000 cavalry spouting "fire, smoke, and brimstone," which is how modern armored cavalry units would appear to a prophet of ancient times. Mention is made and interpreted by some students of the Bible as a recognizable reference to thermonuclear warfare, of the power "to scorch men with fire" and that men were "scorched with great heat and blasphemed the name of God . . ." and of an earthquake "such as was not since men were upon the earth so mighty an earthquake and so great," and that ". . . every island fled away, and the mountains were not found . . ."

There is even a passage in Zechariah 14 which, in describing the effects of a future battle, reads:

> Their flesh shall consume away while they stand upon their feet, and their eyes shall consume away in their holes . . .

a phenomenon familiar to observers of the effect of atomic bombs. Also reminiscent of what one hopes we will avoid in the future is a forewarning contained in the Book of Esdras of the Apocrypha which tells of

> . . . great and mighty clouds . . . shall rise to destroy all the earth and its inhabitants . . . and they shall destroy cities and walls, mountains and hills, trees of the forest and grass of the meadows and their grain . . . no one shall be left to cultivate the earth or to sow it . . .

In the Gospel according to St. Luke and also mentioned by St. Matthew there is a prophecy attributed to Jesus Christ which describes a period wherein "Jerusalem encompassed with armies" will be a sign of the approaching Final Judgment:

When you shall hear of wars and commotions, be not terrified; for these things must first come to pass; but the end is not by and by. Then said he unto them, Nation shall rise against nation, and kingdom against kingdom: and great earthquakes shall be in divers places, and famines, and pestilences; and fearful sights and great signs shall be from heaven. And when ye shall see Jerusalem compassed with armies, then know that the desolation thereof is nigh. And there shall be signs in the sun, and in the moon, and in the stars; and upon the earth distress of nations, with perplexity; the sea and the waves roaring; So likewise ye, when ye see these things come to pass, know ye that the kingdom of God is nigh at hand.

The Biblical prophecies doubtless contributed strongly to the medieval conviction that the world would end with the first millennium. When it did not do so the feeling of relief and thankfulness felt in the European Middle Ages may have encouraged the building of the vast cathedrals which flowered during this era, and no doubt, because of religious fervor, increased the zeal of the subsequent Crusades. Somewhat later, in the early 1350s the Black Death appearing suddenly in Europe and causing the deaths of a third of the population, with resulting breakdown of society and widespread madness, was thought by many, before it abated and life went on, to be the actual end of the world. After this visitation popular belief began to consider that perhaps Doomsday had been postponed, at least until the *second* millennium.

Some of the medieval European prophets made written predictions, often printed at the time, so that one can be fairly sure that they were not predated, that seem to link themselves to the events of today. Sometimes even the future year is specifically mentioned as in the case of Nostradamus who wrote in the middle of the 1500s:

The year one thousand nine hundred and ninety nine,
  the seventh month,
A great frightening king will come from the sky,
To raise the great king of the Angoulmois,
Before and afterwards Mars will reign uninterrupted.

This prediction has been variously interpreted by modern observers, as an atom bomb, a rogue planet, or an air attack, possibly by the Chinese (depending on a cryptic reading of Angoulmois as "Mongol").

Nostradamus, perhaps the best known of the medieval prophets, in realistic consideration of the climate of the time, usually wrote his prophetic quatrains in a somewhat camouflaged fashion to protect himself from accusations of heresy or to avoid political misadventure. His complete predictions were divided into twelve centuries of one hundred verses each, of which many have been lost. But some of those that remain have proved surprisingly accurate, at least if they have been read correctly. Goethe once observed: "Every prophecy made by Nostradamus between 1555 and 1566 pertaining to then and to today has come true." As many of Nostradamus' predictions refer to the politics of his time, it would of course be natural for an observant person like him to make an informed guess that would prove correct (as in the case of today's prophets). It is, nevertheless, something more than startling when a seer of the sixteenth century can accurately and in detail predict events which would take place two to four centuries later, such as the French Revolution, details of Napoleon's career and exile to Elba, events of World War II including the invasion of Europe, the Maginot Line, the initial triumph of Germany, the death of Mussolini, puns on the names of Hitler and Roosevelt, and the use of atom bombs.

Even today in the 1980s some of his predictions are uniquely recognizable by coincidence or design:

A Libyan prince becomes powerful in the West.
France shall be preoccupied with the Arabs.

While the following could easily be interpreted, if
written in our own day, as referring to the troubles of
the Shah of Iran and the revolution directed from
French exile by the Ayatollah Khomeini:

*Copy of a drawing of Nostradamus made shortly after the French
Revolution which he predicted with the approximate date and
unusually convincing details about 240 years before it happened. A
much commented-on prophecy of Nostradamus concerns a catastrophe which will occur on the 9th day of the 9th month of 1999.*

> Rain, hunger, and unceasing war in Persia.
> Excessive faith will betray the king.
> Finishing there—begun in France.

Nostradamus limited the power of the British Empire, *before it started,* to 300 years. The peculiar ability of Nostradamus in predicting details of incidents hundreds of years in advance is especially notable in his description of the capture of Louis XVI by revolutionaries and his being brought back to the Tuileries (not yet constructed) and puns on the names of two participants, hundreds of years before their births. Because of the almost uncanny accuracy of some of his predictions many persons, other than psychics, are watching with considerable interest to see what will happen in the seventh month of 1999. Nostradamus also indicates several other possible dooms or combinations of catastrophes at the end of this millennium such as:

> The world near its last period,
> Saturn will come back again, late.

The reference to Saturn is an interesting one as this will be one of the important planets in the planetary alignment of 1982, at which time some modern astronomers have suggested that the influence that the great planets in allineation will have on the molten tides inside the earth, pushing the rocky tectonic plates together, may set off a series of catastrophic earthquakes, especially on the fault lines. There seems to be an incredible reference to tectonic plates in another quatrain:

> The fire at the center of the earth
> Will make the new city tremble.
> Two great rocks will contend

Against each other for a long time
And then Arethusa* shall color the new river red . . .

One of the most frequently contemplated dooms of modern prophets concerns the rising of the waters of the sea, since climactically or artificially induced melting of considerable portions of the stored ice at the north and south poles would raise sea levels hundreds of feet. This would have specially catastrophic results for the modern world where so many of the great cities are seaports, and so large a portion of the population is clustered on the coastal plains often only a few feet above sea level. Nostradamus, in a letter of dedication written to his son, Caesar, on March 1, 1555, wrote: "Before the universal conflagration there shall happen so many inundations that there shall scarce be any land that shall not be covered by water . . ." In the same letter he seems again to indicate the present millennium as an end of this "revolution" for humanity:

We are now in the seventh millinary which ends all and brings us near the eighth which is where the great God shall make an end of this revolution . . .

His reference to the end of the seventh millennium can be interpreted as the five thousand years between the Biblical Creation and the birth of Christ, with two thousand years added to that to mark the end of humanity as we now know it. He is more definite in his letter to Henri II of France when he specifies the signs by which it will be recognized:

There will be a solar eclipse more dark and gloomy than any since the creation of the world, except after the death of Christ. And it shall be in the month of October that a great movement of the globe will happen, and it will be such that one will think the gravity of the earth

---

* A classic allusion to a spring coming from the earth.

has lost its natural balance and that it will be plunged into the abyss and perpetual blackness of space. There will be portents and signs in the spring, extreme changes, nations overthrown, and mighty earthquakes.

Another seer of the Middle Ages, who lived before Nostradamus and was known to history as Mother Shipton, specialized in writing the future history of England in couplets. She apparently had an unusual ability to foretell developments in countries that had not yet been mapped by Europeans, such as the U.S.A. and Australia, and even to foretell and describe the use of products not yet known in Europe, such as potatoes and tobacco.

As to the catastrophic ending of the world, she seems to have placed it 400 years after her time, adding certain feminine details for future identification, when she rhymes:

> When women dress like men and trousers wear,
> And cut off all their locks of hair,
> When pictures look alive with movements free,
> When ships like fishes swim beneath the sea,
> When men outstripping birds can soar the sky,
> Then half the world, deep drenched in blood,
>   shall die . . .

Mother Shipton apparently claimed that the world would end in 1981 but a publisher of the nineteenth century, republishing some of her rhymes, apparently doctored the 1981 to 1881, thereby causing a near panic until the date was past.

Another strange prophecy of the Middle Ages was that of St. Malachy, an Irish monk who became the Archbishop of Armagh. Malachy's prophecies took the form of a roster of future popes, starting from his time in the first half of the twelfth century and extending to what seems to be the present time. He couched his prophecies in short Latin phrases descriptive of the reigns, origins, or characteristics of each pope, many of them strikingly apt. St. Malachy's roster predicts that the papacy will end with a pope called Peter at a time which, if calculated according to the average papal reign, indicates the end of the second millennium. According to his description of what is apparently Pope Pius XI, there will be six more popes after him before "Peter the Roman" who will be the last and, as the prophecy continues, "the City of the Seven Hills will be destroyed, and the Awful Judge will judge his people." Although St. Malachy died in 1148, his prophecies were not published until about 1595 after they were found in note form in the Vatican archives. Since then, they have often been referred to and their influence may have contributed to a vision attributed to Pope Pius X (who would, according to St. Malachy's prophecy, be the eighth from last pope) in 1909. While he was holding an audience, Piux X fell into a trance. When he recovered he declared, "What I see is terrifying! Will it be myself . . . or my successor . . . the pope will quit Rome and after leaving the Vatican he will have to walk over the dead bodies of his priests."

Others among the world's great religions also specify in their traditions a fateful time in their history occurring in about 2000 A.D., which of course would not occur in their traditional count although in years it comes out the same as the Western system of counting time.

In archaeological and other scientific terms 2000 A.D. is often referred to as 2000 C.E. (common era) and B.C. as B.C.E. (before common era) in an effort to render the scientific count of years more religiously neutral inasmuch as almost all national units now use the calendar whose identifying letters hitherto have stood for "Before Christ" or "In the Year of Our Lord." It is nevertheless remarkable that religions and traditions with no common starting point coincide in their prophecies of a date in Western count 2000 A.D.

which will signify an end or new beginning of humanity.

For example, Buddhist tradition placed the end of the present world at 2,500 years from the birth of Gautama Siddartha, the Buddha, at which time mankind will be redeemed by Maitreya, the future Buddha, and Gautama Siddartha, it may be noted, lived 2,500 years ago.

Tibetan and Mongolian Buddhist tradition had long foretold the end of the rule of the Dalai Lamas and a whole way of life after the reign of the thirteenth. This prophecy was fulfilled, as predicted, with the onrush of Communist troops from China.

Hinduism calculates the age of humanity as the yuga (epoch) of Kali, the Goddess of Destruction, and this is the age now drawing to a close.

The force for preservation in Hindu theogony, Vishnu, has already saved humanity on a number of occasions, symbolically appearing as a savior in the form of a fish, tortoise, boar, man-lion, dwarf, Parashurama (Rama with the ax), Rama, Krishna, and Buddha. He will finally appear, soon, as Kalki, a white horse, destined to destroy the present world and take humanity to a different, higher plane.

In the very heart of Asia, in the deserts of Mongolia and the mountain reaches of Tibet there has existed for many centuries the mysterious and mystical tradition of Arghati and its ruler, the King of the World. Arghati is believed by many to be an actual inner world existing under the high plateau in the mountains of Central Asia, a series of huge caverns with secret entrances to the surface of the earth through which ancient tribes sometimes entered and there continued a hidden civilization down to the present day. This underground Shangri-la is still believed to exist underneath the Communist-dominated surface and whenever its ruler, the King of the World, makes prophecies the birds and animals on the surface of the earth suddenly become silent. Hundreds of years ago the

King of the World made a prophecy which, counting from the time it was purportedly given, falls, as do so many other predictions, within the latter part of the twentieth century.

> Men will increasingly neglect their souls. . . . The greatest corruption will reign on earth. Men will become like bloodthirsty animals, thirsting for the blood of their brothers. The crescent will become obscured and its followers will descend into lies and perpetual warfare. . . . The crowns of kings will fall. . . . There will be a terrible war between all the earth's peoples . . . entire nations will die . . . hunger . . . crimes unknown to law . . . formerly unthinkable to the world. . . . The persecuted will demand the attention of the whole world . . . the ancient roads will be filled with multitudes going from one place to another . . . the greatest and most beautiful cities will perish by fire. . . . Families will be dispersed . . . faith and love will disappear . . . the world will be emptied . . . within fifty years there will be only three great nations . . . Then, within 50 years there will be 18 years of war and cataclysms. . . . Then the peoples of Agharti will leave their subterranean caverns and will appear on the surface of the earth . . .

It is noteworthy that all the ancient predictions of doom, most of them fixing Doomsday within our own era, concern a mixture of final warfare, earthquakes, tempests, worldwide volcanic eruptions, and overwhelming floods. Most of them deal with especially destructive warfare, with perhaps a suggestion that it will be a sign of, or a contribution to, final doom.

Announcements of impending catastrophe are now becoming more frequent; they come not only from modern psychic prophets but from scientists of a variety of disciplines. While the prophetic ability of modern scientists has been immeasurably strengthened by calculations of computers, electronic memories, satellites, space probes, and investigative equipment of which past prophets probably never dreamed, it can still be said that they are the descendents and modern equivalents of the astrologers and necromancers of an earlier era.

And, curiously, the conclusions of some of these coincide with the ancient prophecies.

4

Countdown
to Doom

From the high ziggurats of ancient Mesopotamia, the
spiral winding towers where Babylonian and Assyrian
astrologers studied the stars and planets and planetary
satellites through some means which enabled them to
see stars not visible to the naked eye, to the giant
observatories of today, humanity has been preoccupied with the stars and planets, and their influence on
the earth. The Sumerians, predecessors of the Babylonians, credited Nergal (Mars), the god of war, with
causing earthquakes. They thought that the god
Nergal could move ". . . the earth off its hinges . . .
causing the earth to shudder . . ."

All over the world complicated stone observatories
are the only or principal remains of lost civilizations.
These include the great standing rocks of Stonehenge
on the Salisbury Plain in England, the great zodiacal
circle at Glastonbury, thirty miles in circumference,
the enormous standing bolders of Carnac in France,
and countless other stone circles and star stones
throughout prehistoric Europe. The King's Gallery of
the Great Pyramid of Egypt opens to the sky directly
to the North Star, now in the Great Bear constellation
but in the Dragon when the Pyramid was built.

The ancient Greeks inherited from prior cultures a
considerable amount of astronomical consciousness

but modified it to conform to the actions and escapades of their gods. As Plato remarked in his *Timaeus* dialogue, referring to the near destruction of the earth in prehistoric times:

> . . . this has the form of a myth but really signifies a declination of the bodies moving around the earth and in the heavens, and a great conflagration of things upon the earth recurring at long intervals of time . . .

We also have the macabre Greek legend about Cronus (Saturn) eating his children, which undoubtedly comes from the fact that the planet Saturn covers up its moons periodically, although this activity cannot be seen without a strong telescope, presumably unknown to the Greeks of antiquity.

In the Americas there are great stone star circles of unknown age in the Mojave Desert and other parts of the western states and in Canada. Maya astronomers were preoccupied with the stars, and their observatory at Chichén Itzá, Yucatan, still stands today. In Central America perfectly tooled and rounded stone balls, of sizes varying from small boulders to great monoliths, have been found in the jungles of Costa Rica and San Salvador indicating by their dispersal and arrangement that they may have been part of a gigantic planetarium, showing the position of the stars and planets in Maya, or perhaps earlier times. One of the most sacred spots of the Inca Empire was an opening over a stone enclosure on a mountain top, the Intihuatana—"hitching post of the sun"—where the sun's rays struck exactly once a year only, at the winter solstice. And one of the principal reasons for the prevalent Aztec custom of human sacrifice was to keep the sun, moon, stars, and planets on their correct courses. The priests and astrologers of the ancient cultures did not watch the skies out of idle interest but rather to see what would happen to the world.

Astrology and astronomy may therefore be the first

of the pure sciences, the progenitors of both mathematics and writing. The words themselves, despite the
hint of opprobrium (and, in the Middle Ages, danger)
held by the former, are really essentially the same,
astrology meaning "word of the stars" and astronomy
"arrangement of the stars." Today's astronomers, able
to scan the skies with incredibly far-seeing telescopes,
aided by extensive computer information, satellite reports, and cosmic probes, are now uncovering mysteries unsuspected by their ancient and medieval fore-
bears. Nevertheless, they often still arrive at
conclusions which, transfigured by scientific nomen-
clature, still convey a message well known to the
astrologers of antiquity—namely that the movements
of the heavenly bodies effect our own world.

We are aware, of course, of the effect of the sun and
moon upon the tides of the sea and even the tides of
human consciousness, and we are generally aware that
climatic conditions on the earth are affected by sunspots and the resultant solar wind which bombards the
earth with ionized hydrogen and helium. It has long
been suspected that sunspots have a potentially dangerous effect on Earth's climatic conditions and may
also be connected with seismic activities or earthquakes.

Convincing evidence of the above—a series of great
earthquakes—has been forecast by authors John Gribbin and Stephen Plagemann (*The Jupiter Effect: A
Scientific Exploration of the Planets As Triggers of
Major Earthquakes,* 1974). The target date will be 1982
in December and it will be caused by the allineation
already described. (See illustration, page 49.) The tidal
pull of these planets is projected to cause increased
sunspot activity which, implementing the blast of the
solar wind of charged particles across the earth will
affect the molten inner tides of the globe, especially at
the crucial fault lines which form the plate boundaries,
and shake the earth at its axis, setting off a series of
tremendous earthquakes and volcanic eruptions. Grib-

bin points out that this grand alignment of planets has been selected by numerous astrologers as the beginning of the Age of Aquarius—"When Jupiter aligns with Mars and the moon is in the Seventh House . . . and with the other seven planets of the solar system."

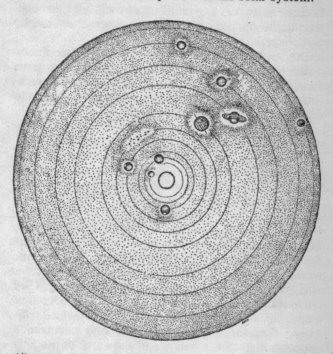

Alignment of the planets around the sun as they are predicted to occur in 1982. Gribbin and Plagemann suggest in The Jupiter Effect *that the tidal pull of these planets may affect the sun flares and thereby the seismic faults and the molten inner tides of Earth, causing devastating earthquakes and perhaps shaking the planet at its axis. Whatever the eventual proof of this theory might be, it is notable that there has been a recent increase in the number of earthquakes and volcanic eruptions, which fits into this theory of coming catastrophe. The planets illustrated, starting next to the Sun, are Mercury, Venus, Earth, Mars, then a presumably missing planet indicated only by an orbiting asteroid belt, followed by Jupiter, Saturn, Uranus, Neptune, and Pluto.*

He suggests, however, that the beginning of the Age of Aquarius may mean the effective end of California as the San Andreas fault (already under increasing strain and long overdue at the breaking point; near Pasadena it suddenly moved nine inches to the west in 1980) will become activated as well as other fault lines throughout the world. Los Angeles and other cities will be demolished.

Drs. Gribbin and Plagemann are not science fiction writers but astronomers and astrophysicists from Cambridge University. Despite their scientific preparation, however, they have the academic courage to observe,

> Now, to the surprise of many scientists, there has come evidence that . . . the astrologers were not so wrong after all: it seems that the alignments of the planets can, for sound scientific reasons, affect the behavior of the earth.

If this prediction of great earthquakes from cosmic tidal effects takes place in 1982 on schedule, then the earth may experience a greater disaster in 2000 A.D. connected with and caused by the even more direct alignment scheduled to take place at that time. (See illustration on page 51.) In the opinion of Dr. Geoffrey Goodman, a geologist and author of *We Are the Earthquake Generation* (1978), this second occurrence might so disturb the balance of the earth on its axis that the great earthquakes, in combination with the increasing weight of ice at the south pole, might cause the earth to flip over in space with catastrophic results for everything living on the face of the earth.

It should be pointed out, however, that while the alignment of the planets in 1982 is astronomically certain and that the last time it happened, 179 years previously, serious earthquakes did occur, there is no positive proof that they will happen this time, or that San Francisco will experience "the Big One" (as it is referred to locally), that Los Angeles will fall into the sea, or that a series of world earthquakes will bring on a global catastrophe.

On the other hand, as the year 1982 approaches, earthquake activity all over the world seems to be intensifying both in number of temblors and in intensity on the Richter scale.

The Richter scale rates earthquakes from 1 to 9, 1 being a light tremor, usually imperceptible, anything over 2 being noticeable to people, and anything over

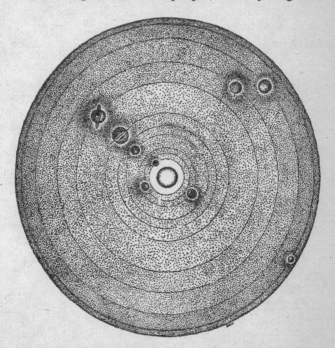

The position of planets calculated to occur in early May 2000, when the pull of their joint alignment is expected by some astronomers, as well as astrologers and psychics, past and present, to cause solar flares on the sun, severe earthquakes and seismic explosions on the Earth, land changes, and even to affect the Earth's rotational balance. For names of orbiting planets compare figure on page 49.

NO.	DATE	LOCALITY	INTENSITY ON RICHTER SCALE
1	1556	T'ai-yuan, Shansi, China	
2	December 31, 1703	Tokyo, Japan	
3	November 1, 1755	Lisbon, Portugal (Algeria, Morocco)	
4	November 1755	Boston, Massachusetts	
5	1783	Calabria, Italy	
6	December 16, 1811	New Madrid, Mo.	
7	1868	Peru-Ecuador	
8	1866	Charleston, South Carolina	
9	April 18, 1906	San Francisco, California	
10	1908	Messina, Italy	
11	December 16, 1920	Kansu, China	
12	September 1, 1923	Yokohama-Tokyo, Japan	
13	February 25, 1925	St. Lawrence Valley	
14	1935	Quetta, Pakistan	
15	1939	Erzincan, Turkey	
16	January 25, 1939	Chillan, Chile	
17	November 16, 1940	Bucharest, Romania	
18	1960	Agadir, Morocco	
19	1963	Skopje, Yugoslavia	
20	1964	Niigata, Japan	
21	1964	Anchorage, Alaska	
22	Oct. 26-27, 1969	Banja Luka, Yugoslavia	8.0
23	May 31, 1970	Santa Valley, Peru	9.0
24	March 28-29, 1970	Gediz, Turkey	8.8

NO.	DATE	LOCALITY	INTENSITY ON RICHTER SCALE
25	January 4-5, 1970	Mangkalan, N. Burma	8.0
26	February 9, 1971	Los Angeles, California	6.3
27	December 23, 1972	Managua, Nicaragua	7.5
28	February 25, 1973	Kurile Islands, U.S.S.R.	8.5
29	November 22, 1975	Hawaii	7.4
30	May 26, 1975	Lisbon, Portugal (Atlantic Ocean)	8.0
31	February 3, 1975	Kaich'eng, China	9.0
32	November 24, 1976	Caldiran, Turkey	7.9
33	July 27, 1976	T'angshan, China	8.6
34	May 17, 1976	Tashkent, U.S.S.R.	9.0
35	May 6, 1976	Bolzano, Italy	7.0
36	May 4, 1976	Guatemala City, Guatemala	7.5
37	August 19, 1977	Seaquake. Sumba, Indonesia	8.9
38	April 1, 1977	Seaquake between Samoa, Tonga	7.5
39	Mar. 21-Apr. 1, 1977	Gulf of Iran (double)	7.0
40	March 4, 1977	Bucharest, Romania	7.5
41	November 5, 1978	Solomon Islands	7.5
42	September 16, 1978	Tabas, Iran	7.7
43	June 20, 1978	Salonika, Greece	7.0
44	June 4, 1978	Turkmen, U.S.S.R.	8.0
45	December 12, 1979	Colombia-Ecuador	8.1
46	September 12, 1979	New Guinea	8.0
47	April 15, 1979	Coast of Yugoslavia	7.8
48	January 1, 1980	Azores	7.0

Map showing within numbered circles locations of the most important and destructive temblors for the past three hundred years, although because of difficulty of communication before 1900, many more presumably happened before that time. But it is evident that within the last few years a considerable increase in earthquakes is taking place, establishing a pattern of seismic activity that seems to be cresting.

4.5 being considered a danger to life and property. A temblor of 8.2 plus is capable of killing hundreds of thousands of people as happened in China in 1976. As temblors are measured in energy released, an 8 quake is not to be considered twice as serious as a 4 but rather thousands of times as intense. It has been calculated that earthquakes measuring 8.6 on the Richter scale represent an energy release comparable to a force 300,000 times that of the first atom bomb used in combat at Hiroshima.

Earthquakes are usually accompanied by volcanic eruptions, if there are volcanoes in the area, as the stresses within the earth seek outlets for their built-up forces. Earthquakes which take place near the sea are usually followed by huge tidal waves as the sea floor is also affected by the earthquake. These tidal waves are almost always presaged by water receding from the shoreline to come back within minutes in a giant *tsunami*, the Japanese word for "port wave" or "harbor wave." The word has been internationally adopted to mean "tidal wave," a disaster so frequent in Japan. Tsunamis, which have sometimes attained the awesome height of 240 feet do not crest until they near the shore; the great tsunami of the 1923 Tokyo-Yokohama earthquake did not capsize ships under steam at sea but sank or wrecked the ships at anchor or docked within the harbor as it crested and swept over Yokohama.

An examination of recorded earthquakes with rat-

	9.R (or above)	8.R (or +)	7.R (or +)	6.R (or +)	5.R (or +)
1974	0	1	6	10	15
1975	1	1	5	10	18
1976	1	1	9	26	35
1977	0	1	11	23	32
1978	0	2	12	22	40
1979	0	4	10	25	41

ings over 5 from 1974 to 1979 gives a fairly clear indication of worldwide increase in frequency and intensity.

As this book goes to press reported earthquakes in 1980 indicate that the number is still increasing impressively as earthquakes continue to happen even in areas hitherto earthquake free. In addition the considerable increase in the number of earthquakes in these years that have measured over 7 on the Richter scale is a clear indication that the intensity of earthquakes is increasing. The 1976 shock in Tangshan, China, which killed between 750,000 to 800,000 people, the biggest single earthquake death toll yet recorded, was given an 8.2 rating on the Richter scale, with a beyond-scale calculated as 11 at its epicenter.

Earthquake activity is most frequent on the fault lines between the tectonic plates of the earth. These are the separate land and sea floor masses that, driven by the molten inner currents of the earth, move over the magma, the inner surface of the globe, and cause earthquakes as they push, grind, or slip over each other along the fault lines. Now, however, temblors occur more frequently in places previously thought to be immune, such as Scotland, Northern England and, in the United States, Missouri, Michigan, Tennessee, Illinois, and Pennsylvania.

The main earthquake zones, along the boundaries of the tectonic plates, can be seen on the map on this page. The semicircular Pacific zone, called the "ring of fire," including Indonesia, Japan, Alaska, California, the west coast of Central and South America, and part of the Caribbean is, with a certain justification, a favorite target for prophets of disaster.

The recent eruptions of Mount Agung, in Bali, Indonesia and Mount St. Helens in Washington State, U.S.A., gave convincing indication of seismic activity within the Pacific "ring of fire." The 1979 eruption of Mount Dieng caused numerous deaths through the emission of poisonous gases. The eruption of Mount

St. Helens, previously quiet for 137 years, which took place on May 18, 1980, has been called the greatest natural explosion in American recorded history. It is thought to have been caused by earthquakes three miles under its cone which introduced gases into the molten rock, the magma of the earth's interior, resulting in an explosion comparable to that of a multimegaton H-bomb, taking 1,300 feet off the top of the mountain, flattening 150 square miles of forest, and killing an estimated 100 persons and unknown quantities of wild life.

The deaths from gas and hot ash, the long-range bombardment of hot rocks, the heavy cloud of smoke, gas, and ash which reached ten miles into the stratosphere, and the flood of ashes covering roads, houses,

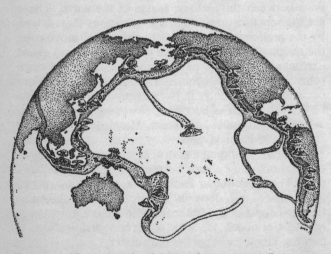

The "ring of fire"—a circle of the Pacific area especially prone to earthquakes and volcanic eruptions. The earthquake zone enclosed in the circling dotted lines roughly follows the boundaries of the tectonic plates of the earth. The sketched-in volcanoes indicate volcanic mountains subject to periodic and some very frequent eruptions.

and people have been made thoroughly familiar to us through TV and press reports.

It is nevertheless interesting to read a former commentator, writing at another time, who has left us a vivid on-the-spot report of a volcano in eruption. Some excerpts from his account are surprisingly applicable to the Mount St. Helens explosion:

> ·The cloud was rising (from the eruption) in appearance and shape it was like a tree . . . an immense tree trunk as it was projected into the air and opened out into branches . . . carried up by a violent gust, sometimes white while sometimes dark and mottled, depending on whether it bore ashes or cinders . . . my uncle struggled to his feet but fell down again immediately. I assume that his breathing was impeded by the dense vapors . . . on the second day his body was found intact . . . there loomed a horrible black cloud ripped by sudden bursts of fire, writhing snakelike and revealing sudden flashes greater than any lightning . . . thick smoke spread over the earth like a flood, following us . . . and then came the ash thick and heavy . . . from time we had to get up and shake the ashes off for fear of being buried under their weight . . . finally daylight came; the sun shone but pallidly, as in an eclipse . . . everything appeared changed—covered by a thick layer of ashes like an abundant snow fall . . .

The above description is taken from a letter about a volcanic eruption which took place many centuries ago. It was written by Pliny the Younger. The uncle who died was Pliny the Elder, a naturalist and an admiral of the imperial Roman fleet. The volcano was Vesuvius, the destroyer of Pompeii and Herculaneum. The date—August 24, 79 A.D.

The catastrophe of Vesuvius, however, did not impede survivors and others from returning to the area and building new towns over the entombed ruins of the former settlements. This same reaction has often been noted in Japan, Northern China, the west coasts of North and South America, the Middle East, Central America and the Caribbean, where, in 1902 a poisonous and scorching gas cloud from the eruption of Mount Pelée killed 28,000 people, the entire population of St. Pierre, Martinique, but did not discourage the rebuilding of the city. This tenacity demonstrates a blend of confidence, optimism, and perhaps fatalism. Fortunately, there are now at hand new means of predicting the dangerous inner tensions of the earth.

Seismologists have made considerable progress in forecasting earthquakes by noting and testing features that seem to announce them. This includes the swelling of subterranean rocks, a change in the chemical content of local water, uplifting of the soil, a sudden change of earth water levels in wells, resistance of rocks to electric currents, and the presence of radon gas in spring water and streams.

It has been noted that there may also exist a natural earth sound warning system. The great boom heard from the north Atlantic coast of the U.S. in 1977–78, which baffled all government agencies and was popularly attributed to everything from a sonic boom to UFOs, may have been caused by subterranean gases released by movements within the lithosphere. In fact, one boom was closely followed by a temblor along the Ramapo fault, located in the Ramapo hills of New Jersey. Unfortunately these warning sounds may constitute a short-fuse warning only—too late for those who hear them to leave the area, as is also the case with the yellow-orange glow often noted in the Andes and other mountainous areas shortly before a temblor.

A general earthquake prediction, agreed upon by most seismologists, is the somewhat obvious one which could be simply stated as follows: if it happened here before, it can happen here again, when the pressure becomes sufficient. But there seems to be a more immediate way, especially for inhabitants of rural districts, to tell in advance when an earthquake is likely to occur. This concerns the behavior of animals, which seem to have instinctive knowledge of approaching earthquakes. In China it has long been noted that, prior to an earthquake, rats scamper from buildings and pigs desperately try to escape from their sties. In Central Asia horses and camels become frantic and unmanageable; in Italy cows and goats panic in the barns; in Japan catfish attempt to leap out of their ponds.

Just before the Anchorage earthquake in Alaska (1964) the great Kodiak bears left their hibernation caves early and went to open ground. It was possible to minimize human fatalities by forewarnings in the Chinese Haicheng quake (1975) when it was noted that great numbers of snakes had crawled out from their winter holes and had frozen to death on the snow and ice. People living in urban earthquake areas who might or might not be in touch with warning systems or are unaware of the reactions of farm or wild animals prior to earthquakes, should note that domestic apartment-dwelling animals are also affected. Cats' fur stands on end, dogs howl inexplicably, goldfish, like their larger relatives in the lakes of Japan, try to leap out of their bowls. At the Stanford Outdoor Primate Facility in California special studies are being made on the reactions of chimpanzees to seismic changes. A Stanford geophysicist, Dr. Amos Nur, has stated that these animal behavior studies "will comprise the most important single effort in earthquake prediction during the next few years" (Don DeNevi, *Earthquakes:* 1977).

Perhaps animals have senses that most people have lost. It may be that psychics, with their increased sensitivity and extrasensory perception, are examples of humans who have developed this capacity to predict catastrophic events not only in the immediate future but sometimes years before the event occurs.

If this is possible Edgar Cayce, perhaps the best

known of modern psychics and clairvoyants, is one of these. Cayce, who between 1901 and 1945 gave thousands of trance "readings" unusually accurate in medical advice and social, political, and even geophysical predictions, is an excellent example of what we may call a natural prophet—one who prophesied without plan or hope of personal gain. Many of his prophecies, made well in advance of the event, have come true. These include the prediction that a coming president would be *the second one* not to live through his term of office (this was after Franklin Roosevelt); civil and racial strife in the United States; the behavior of the stock market; the use of laser and maser beams (unknown at the time he described them); the discovery of prehistoric ruins on the ocean floor near Bimini; all these predictions were made decades before the events took place. An example of just one of his prophecies made over thirty-nine years ago requires very little interpretation to realize its pertinence now, in 1980:

Strife will arise through the period. . . . Watch for them in Libya and in Egypt, and in Syria. Through the straits around these areas above Australia; in the Indian Ocean and the Persian Gulf . . .

Cayce has furnished us with an awesomely detailed account of what earthquakes, volcanic eruptions, and catastrophic modifications of the earth's surface we can expect in the latter half of the twentieth century. The paragraphs quoted below are partial sections from some of his readings.

His prediction of changes in the land and sea structure of the earth follow what we may call a timetable of catastrophe from 1958 to the second millennium to be introduced by violent activity in the Etna area and the rising and sinking of sea levels in the Mediterranean, both of which have already happened. He detailed some of the next scheduled changes:

The earth will be broken up in many places. The early portion will see a change in the physical aspect of the west coast of America. There will be open waters appearing in the northern portions of Greenland. There will be new lands seen off the Caribbean Sea, and DRY land will appear . . . South America shall be shaken from the uppermost portion to the end, and in the Antarctic off Tierra del Fuego, LAND, and a strait with rushing waters.

The earth will be broken up in the western portion of America.

The greater portion of Japan must go into the sea. The upper portion of Europe will be changed as in the twinkle of an eye.

There will be upheavals in the Arctic and the Antarctic that will make for the eruptions of volcanos in the Torrid areas and there will be the shifting then of the poles—so that where there have been those of frigid or semi-tropical will become the most tropical and moss and ferns will grow . . .

In 1941 Cayce, while in a trance-sleep, answered the following implied question:

Question: I have for many months felt that I should move away from New York City.

Cayce: This is well, as indicated. There is too much unrest; there will continue to be the character of vibrations that to the body will be disturbing, and eventually those destructive forces there—though these will be in the next generation.

Question: Will Los Angeles be safe?

Cayce: Los Angeles, San Francisco, most all of these will be destroyed before New York even.

In 1936 Cayce indicated that future volcanic explosions from Vesuvius and Peleé (in Martinique) would be the signal that a flood—or tidal wave—would sweep

over the southern coast of California as far east as
Utah and Nevada. Even more disquieting predictions
followed:

> Many portions of the east coast will be disturbed, as
> well as many portions of the west coast, as well as the
> central portion of the United States.

> In the next few years, lands will appear in the Atlan-
> tic as well as in the Pacific. And what is the coast line
> now of many a land will be the bed of the ocean. Even
> many of the battlefields of the present (1941-45) will be
> ocean . . .

> Portions of the now east coast of New York, or New
> York City itself, will in the main disappear. This will be
> another generation, though, here: while the southern
> portions of Carolina, Georgia, these will disappear.
> This will be much sooner . . .

Cayce was asked in 1932 how soon these changes in
the earth's surface would become apparent. He replied:

> When there is the first breaking up of some conditions
> in the South Sea and those as apparent in the sinking
> and rising of that almost opposite the same or in the
> Mediterranean and the Etna area. Then we will know it
> has begun.

A clue may have been given on September 17, 1979
when a very powerful earthquake, 8.0 on the Richter
scale—occurred at Ansus and other towns on Yapen
Island in Indonesia. On the same afternoon the top of
Mount Etna, in Sicily, "exploded like a cannon,"
killing some tourists engaged in climbing what they
had considered to be a safe volcano. It is to be noted
that Mount Etna is on the opposite side of the world
from Indonesia.

Finally one is reminded of the spiritual *and* scientific

coincidence of the feeling that something extraordinary is due to take place in 2000 A.D. as we read an exchange recorded in 1936:

> *Question:* What great change or the beginning of what change, if any, is to take place on the earth in the year 2000 to 2001 A.D.?
>
> *Cayce:* When there is a shifting of the poles. Or a new cycle begins.

Skeptics might point out, in considering some of Edgar Cayce's predictions of land changes on the west coast of the United States that, in a region noted for earthquakes like California such prophecies might be relatively easy to make. What is more noteworthy, therefore, was Cayce's insistence on a period of increasing volcanic eruptions on the west coast from 1958 to 2000 (*Land Changes:* 1959. NB: Cayce died in 1955), with previously safe volcanoes bursting into activity. The May, 1980 eruption of Mount St. Helens, followed by temblors at Mammoth Lake in the Californian Sierras (6 on the Richter scale) and other shocks at San Francisco, San Diego, and Las Vegas (5 to 5.5 Richter), might give rise to second thoughts on the part of observers about the prophecies of Cayce in connection with the whole series of volcanoes on the west coast of the United States, including Mount Baker, Mount Rainier, Mount Adams, Mount Hood, Crater Lake, Mount Shasta, and Lassen Peak. Up to now these "safe" volcanoes have been relatively quiet although still possessing an inner life indicated by occasional spurts of ash and eruptions of steam. One remembers that all these peaks are a part of the great volcanic "ring of fire" formed by the grinding boundaries of the tectonic plates in the great circle around the Pacific Ocean.

The late Hugh Auchincloss Brown was not a psychic but an electrical engineer and scientific investigator, with an *idée fixe* that he pursued for a lifetime with

crusading zeal. This was that the earth would soon
approach a shift in its axis caused by a concentration
of ice on the south pole. The earth, of course, already
has a certain imbalance in its rotation, the Chandler
Wobble (possibly associated with earthquakes caused
by fluid shiftings at the earth's inner core). But Brown
claimed that, because of the increasing weight of ice in
Antarctica, the earth is like a "top-heavy, dying out,
wobbling, spinning top, getting ready to fall over on its
side."

This author, while researching material for *Mysteries from Forgotten Worlds,* became acquainted with
Brown in 1971, when Brown was ninety-two years old,
still actively compiling proof that the excessive pressure of ice at the south pole would cause the axial
poles to move away from the poles of spin with the
result that the earth would flip over in space and start a
new spin axis with change of polar locations and
almost completely fatal results to mankind and civilization. The word "almost" however, indicates that
there would be some survivors who would eventually
build up other civilizations until presumably the earth
flipped over once again. This theory would explain the
seeming evidence that there have been on this planet
extensive and advanced civilizations prior to ours.
Because of the catastrophic polar shift their memories
have been preserved only by certain race memories
and artifacts that lie at the bottom (or under the
bottom) of the sea, or under ice, mud, sand, or earth
strata.

Brown, in a phrase combining science and poetry,
refers to the present ice caps on Antarctica as "merely
the last of many that have previously existed . . . the
successor to a long lineage of glistening assassins of
former civilizations on this planet" and expresses his
certainty of "a future world cataclysm during which
most of the earth's population will be destroyed like
the mammoths of prehistoric times. Such an event has
occurred each time that one or two polar ice caps (has)

grown to maturity—a recurrent event in global history clearly written in the rocks of a very old earth."

According to Brown, the immediate urgency of this theory lies in the still increasing volume of the south polar ice cap, whose weight, he calculated at the time he wrote his main book on the subject *(Cataclysms of the Earth:* New York, 1967) was 19 quadrillion tons, getting heavier with each succeeding year since the earth started rotating at the present axis of figure 7,000 years ago. The ice is now 14,000 feet above sea level and its awesome weight is pushing a declivity (or "ice bowl") into the land beneath it, making room thereby for still more ice.

Brown felt that the next polar flip would take place in the near future or was already overdue. And when we consider the increasing number of earthquakes at the present time and the possible pull at the inner tides of the earth, and stress on tectonic plates which have been predicted as starting in 1982 with the planetary alignment, we detect an additional urgency which Brown had not even considered.

For years he was preoccupied by the need to awaken public consciousness to the danger implicit in the Antarctic ice cap. He was in constant contact with scientific and geological organizations and attempted unsuccessfully to interest the United States government in a prevention project. He died in 1976 still worrying about the ice cap which "if left uncontrolled by man, this wanton titanic power is ready, able, and destined to end our civilization." It might be observed that the melting, if feasible, should not be too rapid, for too speedy melting would flood the coastlands of the world, an eventuality which would also happen if the world weather became warmer by only several degrees. One suggestion might be the proposed supplying of water and irrigation of desert lands in Arabia, Africa, the Middle East and other deserts by towing enormous freshwater icebergs or separating and transporting large chunks from the ice mass to parched regions as potential water supplies. This project has already been under consideration although not for Brown's reasons.

Meanwhile the "glittering assassin" grows larger and higher every year. Admiral Byrd established a base in Antarctica in 1930, and since that time the ice floor has reached past his 110-foot radio towers so that just a few feet now protrude above the icy surface. By the end of this millenium, or perhaps sooner, we may have ascertained the correctness of Brown's theory.

An interesting alternate theory regarding the numerous catastrophes produced by the shifting of the earth's poles has been developed by the research of many years of Charles Hapgood, science professor at Keene College, New Hampshire, who, in his book *Earth's Shifting Crust* (Philadelphia, 1958) proposes that the poles have changed position many times in the past. Each time this has caused great climatic changes, tidal waves and floodings, extinction of species and, for humanity, the disappearance of populations and even civilizations. In Hapgood's words:

> The repeated upheavals of earth and rising and falling of the seas and changes of climate destroyed a world wide ancient civilization culturally superior to and situated in different locations from those that we customarily recognize as the first civilizations of antiquity.

According to Hapgood's theory, polar displacement comes from a shift in the tides of the molten magma within the earth, perhaps aided by the lateral rotational pull caused by the increasing weight of the ice cap at the south pole. Neither the tides nor the increasing wobble of the earth will cause the earth to fall over on its axis, as in Brown's theory, but rather to pull the lithosphere, the surface plates that make up the outer skin or shell of the earth, into a new position, somewhat as if the loose skin of a tangerine slipped around the fruit and settled at a different location. The axis of rotation stays the same, still with its alternating increasing and decreasing wobble, and also, as has been discovered since 1900, still another phenomenon. Apparently the earth not only wobbles on its axis, it also trembles (nutation) as it spins through the cosmos.

Professor Hapgood theorizes that there have been three polar displacements within the last 100,000 years: once when the north pole moved from the Yukon district of Canada to the Greenland Sea, and again when it moved to Hudson Bay, and the third time when it moved from there to its present location. With the last one ending about 12,000 years ago, it is a theory especially pleasing to partisans of the lost continent of Atlantis, considering that the time Plato gave for the submerging of the legendary lost continent coincides with this estimate. Hapgood thinks it possible that geodetic information presently indicates that a new shift may be starting now, pointing out that the north pole moved ten feet in the period between 1960 to 1968, eight times faster than it did from 1900 to 1960. When the crust moves at a fast rate it develops stresses; fissures and chasms open and tremendous volcanic activity occurs. Along with the activity of forces within the earth climatic changes occur—cyclones, unusual storms and weather conditions, and great tidal waves.

Results of some recent earthquakes may cause even more rapid changes in the shifting crust as the principle of balancing out weights on the revolving earth (isostasis) continues to operate. A recent Chilean earthquake raised parts of Chile's coastline up a thousand feet and a similar phenomenon occurred in Alaska. In 1950 an earthquake in the Himalayas raised parts of the range 100 feet in height even though the Himalayas were already 600 feet too high for isostatic balance. These new and excessive weights on different parts of the planet may well indicate additional seismic shiftings as we approach the crucial period ahead.

Hapgood based his location of polar areas on the

distribution of polar and glacial ice at different identifiable times in the world's geological history, estimating that there have been at least 200 shifts in the earth's crust since the Cambrian period (the first geological period), a method which has subsequently been further confirmed by studies of geomagnetism.

One of the more dramatic proofs used to substantiate sudden climatic changes has been the discovery of great bone yards of animals now extinct who evidently died in a great natural holocaust caused by a sudden and disastrous change of climate. Many of these communal graveyards are found in northern regions where the animals could not have lived unless the climate was considerably warmer. A favorite example, used by Professor Hapgood and many others including Immanuel Velikovsky, is the Berezovka mammoth found quick-frozen in Siberia in 1901, the contents of whose stomach indicated that the animal had been eating temperate zone plants no longer growing in the area where it had been frozen. Actually it was found that he still had buttercups in his mouth which he had been enjoying at the moment of his untimely end.

The famous Berezovka mammoth, complete with hide and hair, can be seen in a Leningrad museum, and is but one of many examples found in the past and still being found in Siberia and North China. Although many mammoths have been found in fields of skeletons (Chinese ivory carvings have been coming from this frozen source for thousands of years), unknown numbers have been discovered in a frozen state with the meat still palatable to dogs and, in one case, served to scientists at a banquet in Moscow. Prior to the banquet the scientists did not know what they were to be served but, according to reports, they found the meat moderately palatable.* An indication of the num-

---

* Meat from a 40,000-year-old frozen horse found in the Alaskan permafrost was served on toast as an *hors d'oeuvre* at an Explorers' Club banquet in New York City in 1972. According to Dr. Valentine, the explorers went back for "seconds."

ber of mammoths found protruding from frozen earth over the centuries can be traced from the word itself. The word "mammoth" comes from the Tartar word "mamont" meaning "earth" since Tartar tribesmen, often encountering the carcasses half buried in the earth, concluded that the great beasts still were living under the earth in burrows.

But the epic of the frozen mammoth may not be over. Through use of a well-preserved body of a young mammoth recently found in Siberia, Soviet medical scientists, according to recent press reports, hope to reactivate long frozen sperm and eventually to reproduce a living mammoth. One might suggest that this has elements of cosmic humor: at a time when future earth changes are threatened, scientists are attempting to re-create a victim of the last cataclysm.

Besides certain scientific warnings of future doom (and rumblings from the earth itself) present-day psychics from various parts of the world seem to share premonitions of a coming disaster. Such well-known American psychics as Jeane Dixon and her one-time biographer and fellow seer, Ruth Montgomery, to mention two examples among many, prophesy the ending of the present world in the relatively near future.

A rather startling observation by Dixon (considering the present population pressure on the environment) made in January, 1978 stated that

. . . overpopulation of the planet in this century was not going to be a problem. Something literally earth shattering occurs . . . a natural phenomenon which, I believe, will be divine intervention, something like a meteor. It will happen in a matter of minutes and will involve the shifting of the waters . . .

She is also quoted in Montgomery's book, *A Gift for Prophecy* (New York, 1965), as predicting a world holocaust in 1999, a date strikingly reminiscent of Nostradamus.

In general, the other modern psychics who foresee a global catastrophe coming with the second millennium differ only in details of the approaching disaster. A number of these psychics have been interviewed in a sort of psychic poll—some on the west coast of the United States by John White, *Pole Shift!* (1980), others in different parts of the country by Geoffrey Goodman, and still others in the United States and overseas by the author.

Many of these prophecies closely follow the scientific predictions of probable disasters along fault lines and volcanic areas that have been made concerning the "ring of fire" around the Pacific where earthquakes triggered by the grinding tectonic plates and resultant volcanic eruptions and tidal waves will allegedly and within the next ten to fifteen years cause catastrophic effects in China and Indonesia (where the Krakatoa volcano, which erupted in 1883 causing 36,000 deaths in West Java, will once again erupt) and tidal waves which will cover great parts of southern India and Bangladesh. Submerged land will rise to the surface in the Indian Ocean in the vicinity of the undersea plateau where the theoretical continent of Gondwanaland is thought to have been located. Great seaquakes and earthquakes will herald the sinking of Japan as well as of Hawaii and New Zealand.

Forecasts for Europe are equally dramatic. Giant temblors are predicted for Scandinavia and the British Isles (a rare earthquake shook northern Britain in early 1980). Parts of England and Scotland will sink beneath the sea and London will become a port on the North Sea.

Copenhagen will be submerged and also large parts of Belgium and the Netherlands. Conversely extensive new land will rise to the east of England. (This land area existed until fairly recent geological times as has been indicated by the finding of numerous prehistoric tools on the bottom of the North Sea and submerged walls and buildings off the sea coast of Germany.) The Mediterranean, the scene of future ruinous earthquakes, to be announced by a tremendous eruption of Mount Vesuvius, will become landlocked, as Gibraltar is again joined to Africa as it was in prehistoric times. Lands will rise from the ocean bottom west of Spain where, according to legend, the pleasant and fertile island of Atlantis once existed some days' sail from the west coast of Hispania.

These European geological upheavals will be contemporaneous with or shortly after the North American seismic convolutions which will destroy New York, Los Angeles, parts of the eastern and western seaboards, open an oceanic sea in the southwest, cause the Greak Lakes to flow southward into the Gulf of Mexico, and widen the St. Lawrence to the point that Montreal and other riverine cities will be drowned.

In South America, parts of the west coastal lands of Peru, Ecuador, Colombia, and Central America will subside under the ocean. The Panama isthmus will split, and one is reminded of the ancient legend of Central American Indian tribes that the two oceans will meet and flow one to the other. As a counterpoint to the sinking and breaking up of parts of the New World, new lands will appear off the coast of California and the west coast of South America. In the western Atlantic, close to Georgia and Florida and within the Caribbean, extensive submerged lands will break the surface whereon will be found traces that they were previously inhabited by tribes and nations unknown to us.

Psychics as well as tectonic scientists are somewhat incongruously united in an "earthquake watch" for developments around the "ring of fire" in the fear that, as they unfold, the other predictions will occur on

schedule. Within the past few years the fact that the
rumbling and violent shaking of the earth is increasing
is apparent to any reader of the daily press. New lands
have risen from the sea floor (Surtsey in Iceland), new
volcanoes have arisen (Mexico and Iceland), and the
volcano and earthquake zones around the Pacific seem
to be rumbling into action.

To an interested observer this concurrence of psychic prescience with a much publicized if far from
general scientific theory, suggests possible reciprocal
influence, dating back perhaps hundreds or thousands
of years to our racial memory of past disasters and the
expectation that there will be more in the future. This
is especially applicable to such a conveniently placed
year, 2000 A.D., where religious and traditional impli-
cations combine with newly discovered scientific
trends. And, while on the subject of religion and belief,
one remembers that science has frequently been called
a new religion, containing as it does, elements of faith,
conflicting dogmas, mystery, and salvation.

While it is, of course, easier for most persons to
accept the convictions of physicists rather than those
of psychics, it is hard to avoid an uneasy feeling that
some psychics, perhaps by a process that we do not
understand today but which will become clearer to us
when we understand more about the subconscious and
perhaps time itself, are able to experience, or sense, in
varying degrees, certain future events. This has been
fairly convincingly shown in some of Cayce's prophecies with more that will be tested by future events and
strikingly illustrated in the predictions of Jeane Dixon.
Dixon, as most people interested in prophecy will
remember, predicted in 1957 an assassination in office
of a blue-eyed president who would be *elected in 1960*.
Previously, she had correctly foretold Gandhi's death
by assassination. In 1968 she foretold that Martin
Luther King would be killed and "Robert Kennedy
will be next," repeating this 1968 prophecy about
Kennedy later in the same year, on May 28 in a

conference at the Ambassador Hotel, Los Angeles, *one week* before Kennedy was assassinated while leaving the hotel via the kitchen exit after delivering a speech in the Ambassador ballroom. She foretold the destruction of a space capsule in 1967 and the deaths of the astronauts. (Test model 204 burned on its pad on January 27, 1967, with astronauts Grissom, White, and Chaffee on board.)

Of course, many successful predictions can be said to be founded on the seer's perceptive ability and historical judgment, such as Heinrich Heine's. More than a century before World War II, he made a certainly accurate prediction that "a drama will be performed in Germany which will make the French Revolution seem like a dainty idyll . . ." The historian H. G. Wells missed prophesying the outbreak of World War II by one year but placed it correctly in Poland, though at a Danzig railroad station. How did the military commentator Homer Lee know, thirty-two years before it happened, that the Japanese would invade the Philippines from the Lingayen Gulf and, by a pincer movement, cut off U.S. forces at Corregidor? Or how did it occur to Jules Verne to make the dimensions of the fictional *Nautilus* the same as those of the United States atomic submarines, more than 150 years before the building of the latter? Why did he choose the coast of Florida, site of the real moon shot, for his fictional moon shot? And, strangest of all, how did he estimate that the fictional *Nautilus* would take 73 hours and 13 minutes to travel from the earth to the moon? (The real Apollo 11 took 73 hours and 10 minutes to reach the spot for its first moon orbit.) These examples of predictions, however curiously exact, are nevertheless explainable by the ability of the originators to make a controlled guess.

But Cheiro's warning to Lord Kitchener, a warning that if taken could have changed the course of history—was that, too, a guess? This amazing warning, made in 1894 (twenty-two years in advance of the event), by Cheiro (the professional name of Count Louis Hamon) to Lord Kitchener informed the famous British general that he should avoid all travel by sea in 1916. If he did not, Cheiro said, he would encounter disaster. In 1916 Lord Kitchener, entrusted because of his prestige with a special mission to keep Imperial Russia operative in World War I, ignored Cheiro's warning and met his death when his ship, the HMS *Hampshire,* hit a German mine and sank at sea, exactly as predicted.

Many famous and successful psychics have encountered in dreams, sleep, intensive prayer, or semitrance a state in which predictions seem to become manifest to them. Edgar Cayce was able quite simply to put himself in such a trance state, and hold conversations and answer questions he could not remember on waking. Nostradamus used a combination of astrology and reflective prayer to obtain information, as he wrote, "for the common benefit of mankind concerning the things that the Divine Essence has revealed to me by astronomical revelation . . ." And in another passage: "I find . . . by my revelations which agree with the Divine Inspiration . . ." The foregoing is in accord with St. Thomas Aquinas' opinion that "a vision of future events is a direct influence from God." A modern Trappist monk quoted in *A Gift for Prophecy* expresses the thought that the power of foresight "still exists in a latent dormant state in all of us and manifests itself spontaneously under certain conditions and situations."

In any event, however the state is arrived at, when we approach the problem of true foresight we are dealing with time itself, and whether time moves straight ahead, which is comforting to contemplate, or whether it is curved or omnipresent at different levels, some of us have been able now and in the past momentarily to penetrate the time curtain, retaining only a quick impression of what we have seen. It is not difficult to consider time as a dimension, which it is, and to realize that we are literally walking through the past in our present activities, through places where forests were growing, animals of all epochs roamed or grazed, buildings existed, people lived, history was acted out, wars were being fought, and all of these activities are still going on, if we were able to view them, according to the speed of light and the distance from which the earth could be viewed in different parts of the universe. And as we walk unconcerned through buildings, people, and events of the past, in a concept of continuous ever present time, so people of the future are walking with equal unconcern through our surroundings and through *us*.

The most important part of time to us, of course, is the *here-now* and also the near future, and it seems illogical to us to consider any other sort of time, although we are aware that if space travelers could approach the speed of light in their flights they would eventually come back to earth considerably younger than their earthbound families, who would have aged by earth time and not by the space speed-of-light time.

At all event, our formerly reliable concept of time going forward is being increasingly questioned in new concepts of time and space, as one realizes when reading Lance Morrow's suggestion that some light dimly seen in space may be "starlight from a future universe, its time flowing in an inverse direction from ours."

The widespread consensus among physics and prophets concerning future events from the 1980s to the year 2000 may, if the events transpire in the way they have been predicted and a world catastrophe does occur, mark a breakthrough in modern prophecy and, in a sense, in the very concept we hold of time. Perhaps psychics, through a mystical projection of their subconscious have crossed, however imperfectly, a time barrier that may not really exist. Perhaps the concept of an ageless and boundless universe may extend in more directions and dimensions than we have hitherto supposed. As has been cogently observed:

Beneath the tides of time and sleep, strange fish are moving.

5

Menace from the Cosmos

The observation made by Professor George Wald of Harvard University that, "It has taken the earth four and a half billion years to find out how old it is" might be extended to "and to find out where it is and what are the dangers to its continued existence." It is only comparatively recently that we, dwellers on the earth, have been able to calculate its age (in the neighborhood of four and a half billion years), its position (within a minor solar system far from the center of the Milky Way galaxy), and, finally, to assess the dangers that it may be facing now or may face in the foreseeable future. Some of these dangers are natural to the cosmos while others may prove to be of our own doing and avoidable if we can control our destructive proclivities.

The 1979 disintegration and fall of Skylab 2 caused considerable apprehension in the various parts of the world in its path, although computerized information had established that there was only a one in six hundred million chance that it would hit someone as it fell from space.

The fear of known or unknown objects falling from the sky is probably an inherited dread, a memory from prehistoric and historic times of meteors and comets, one of which could possibly be big enough to end the earth's existence. This has frequently been predicted throughout history and, in past centuries, has caused panic to reach a crescendo whenever a large comet came near the earth. At the present time we suspect that comets are mostly vapor and frozen particles or snow—a sort of cosmic snowball. It is however believed by some astronomers that there may be an iron core at the oncoming end of the comet, a possibility that can be more closely investigated when the periodically returning Halley's Comet, due in about 1986, will be met in space by an investigative spacecraft sent up by the United States.

Meteors and asteroids, being more solid than comets, cause an explosive and severe impact on the planetary bodies with which they collide, as witnessed by the great craters on the moon, Mercury, Mars and the moons of Mars, Venus, Saturn, and Jupiter. Earth is protected to a certain degree from cosmic missiles by its magnetic field and its atmosphere, the great air sea at the bottom of which we live, and is also protected from solar or other radiation by its ozone layer. Many of the meteors that would cause the earth's surface to be pitted like that of the moon burn up much of their rock and iron content as they enter the atmosphere and therefore rarely hit people, although possibly 2,000 meteors enter the earth's atmosphere every day. Some people in fact have been hit by what later proved to be a small meteor while others among us may have been hit by meteors burned out to pebble or stone size, without even recognizing that we had been hit by a cosmic projectile. (An astronomer from Argentina has calculated that, under the present diffusion of people throughout the world, the average person has a three to ten chance of being struck by a meteor at some time in his or her life.)

But, despite its protective atmosphere, the earth has often been struck by gigantic meteors, some of which have left great circular indentations in the surface which later, filled with water or covered with vegetation, formed depressions more easily recognized from the air than from the ground. We have visual proof of some of these huge meteor strikes; the Meteor Crater in Arizona, Canada's Deep Bay Crater, and Clearwater Lake, the Nasta Poka Islands of Hudson Bay (and perhaps Hudson Bay itself), and the Gulf of St. Lawrence. In other parts of the world the huge Ries Kessel crater in Central Europe, the declivity of the Western Sahara and the Vredefort Dome in South Africa, a series of meteor craters in Australia and Siberia and, in the sea, the possibility that the Gulf of Mexico was formed by a huge asteroid striking the earth.

While it is assumed that none of these large asteroid collisions occurred in historic times, the legend of great fireballs which shook the world have come down to us in a variety of semimythical reports from different races in all the inhabited continents. The Biblical account of the destruction of Sodom and Gomorrah has sometimes been attributed to an asteroid which struck the area and left a crater filled up with the waters of the Red Sea. Even the destruction of the legendary Atlantis has been ascribed to a gigantic meteorite. This theory, proposed by the late German physicist Otto Muck (*Alles über Atlantis:* 1976) suggests that a chance collision of a giant asteroid or small planet with the earth may have destroyed with one blow the central portion of a world culture base in the Atlantic Ocean, causing a worldwide regression of civilization to varying degrees of barbarism and then the slow progress of humanity up to a new civilization, our own, which remembers nothing of the past one except perhaps a version of its name. Professor Muck, by comparing the dates of the beginning of the Mayan calendar with other early astronomical records, thought he had even found a date for the asteroid striking the Atlantic island—June 5, 8498 B.C. at 8 P.M. (Atlantis time). Muck points out the thousands of small oval bays in South Carolina and Georgia and other indentations on the sea floor as well as paleovolcanic evidence in the area as an indication of a great meteorite shower which, in his opinion, accompanied the asteroid as it crashed into the earth in the western Atlantic Ocean.

The largest collection of asteroids within our own solar system orbit the sun in an asteroid belt located between the planets Mars and Jupiter. One of them, Ceres, is 470 miles in diameter, while others vary in size and are estimated to number over 50,000. Over 200 years ago Johann Bode, Director of the Berlin Observatory, developed a theory that suggested that this vast collection of asteroids was all that was left of an exploded planet, whose remains still followed its original path around the sun. His theory was based on taking the distance from the earth to the sun as a basic astronomical unit and adapting it to a progression series of 0, 3, 6, 12, 24, 48, 96, 192, etc. to which he added 4 to each number and then divided by 10, giving .4, .7, 1.0, 1.6, 2.8, 5.2, 10.0, 19.6, etc. These figures and fractional figures multiplied by the basic astronomical unit—the mean distance from the earth to the sun (92,960,000 miles)—all give the approximate distance from the sun of Mercury, Venus, Mars, Saturn, and another unknown but suspected planet and then Uranus. This is either an incredible coincidence or simply an expression of mathematical laws of a cosmic nature. (The two most distant planets, Neptune and Pluto, missed the predicted distance by being closer than suspected, although the discovery of Uranus which fitted conveniently into Bode's Law seemed to be conclusive proof of its application to the other eight planets, including the missing one.)

The questions raised by the missing or destroyed planet are intriguing: Was it destroyed by a cosmic collision with another planet or a giant asteroid? Did original planetary material on the orbital path never succeed in forming a planet in the first place? Or did it, after developing life similar to Earth's and gradually attaining civilization, finally achieve a nuclear potential and blow itself up, destroying itself and leaving great meteor scars on its sister planets and their moons?

If the large declivities throughout the earth are caused by asteroids, which may themselves be pieces of former planets, from our own or other solar systems, there should be a metal core or a variety of metal cores traceable within the craters. This was found to be the case with a meteor crater in Arizona where the iron core was finally located by drilling well under the surface, not in the center but off to the side because of the trajectory of the strike. Over the Gulf of St. Lawrence magnetic anomalies have been noted as well as in other areas of the world where there may be concentrated iron deposits beneath the ground or the sea resulting from falls of meteors. In Mexico, in an area called the "Zone of Silence" in Durango, electromagnetic deviations are so pronounced that radio transmissions do not pass through the area. And in Oregon magnetic variations are so strong that at one place cars left in neutral gear go uphill on their own. And if, as Muck thought, a giant asteroid or showers of asteroids fell on the western Atlantic, driving great islands into the sea, then large concentrations of meteoric iron would lie directly under the sea bottom. This might constitute one explanation of the spinning compasses and other electromagnetic aberrations so long reported by air and sea pilots within the Bermuda Triangle, which occupies to a great extent the supposed site of the lost island continent.

According to the calculations of Dr. Robert Dietz, a noted American geologist, if an asteroid the size of Icarus should hit the earth it would do so with an impact equivalent to a 200-million megaton nuclear blast, a force amply sufficient to sink large islands, set off volcanoes, cause enormous earthquakes, interrupt the earth's magnetic field, and temporarily knock it off its axis. Dr. Dietz has also expressed the opinion that, on a general average, major chunks of space material hit planet Earth once every 10,000 years. If this calculation is correct and the last major land and sea change happened about 11,000 years ago, one might suspect that a cosmic rendezvous for Earth may even now be in preparation at some point in the galaxy.

Icarus, the asteroid that orbits closest to the sun, also comes rather close, in cosmic terms, to the earth from time to time as it accomplishes its great sweeping and eccentric orbit around the sun. (The last time it approached Earth with somewhat uncomfortable closeness was in 1968, and the next time will be in 1983.) The possibility of the earth being struck by a gigantic heavenly body is sometimes cited by modern prophets of catastrophe who interpret Nostradamus' prediction of doom "in 1999" through the appearance of a "new king from the sky" as referring to a comet, planetoid, or giant meteor that will strike the earth.

The prospect of a potentially fatal heavenly body approaching within our planet's gravitational pull in the near future is not a comfortable one to contemplate. There are no such encounters foreseeable at present on the cosmic horizon. A circling planetoid within our system would first have to be pulled or jolted out of its orbit and into Earth's gravitational field unless it was already approaching through space on a fairly direct trajectory as is the case with the thousands of meteors that hit Earth's protective atmospheric shield every day.

There is, however, one cosmic neighbor whose unusual orbit brings it rather close to the earth. This is the somewhat erratic planetoid Toro, first officially observed in 1964 and observed again more closely in 1972. In its orbit it makes five loops between Venus and the earth and then a loop around the earth and is expected back close to the earth in the early 1980s. If it were pushed off its orbit through forces arising from the planetary allineations of 1982 or 2000, it might, in the opinion of some observers, crash into Venus or the earth.

The possible collision with Earth of this planetoid "5 kilometers in diameter" would mean not only the immediate destruction of the strike area but would have undetermined effects on the planetary spin which is already undergoing a considerable wobble. Planning for the protection of Earth from such a catastrophe has already taken place in 1968 at MIT with the establishment of a project purporting to deviate the planetoid from its path or destroy such a planetary intruder. In any case recent collisions have affected the earth only minimally except perhaps for the still unexplained crash or explosion of what is called the Tunguska meteorite.

On June 30, 1908, at about 7:15 A.M. something very big exploded in the sky over a Siberian area between the Chunya and Tunguska rivers, tributaries of the Yenisei, about seventy miles north-west of Vanavara, in what is now the Evenki National Okrug of the Russian SSR, U.S.S.R. The explosion of this object, although calculated to have a diameter of between 30 to 120 feet and therefore not comparable to the erratic Toro mentioned above, was nevertheless strong enough to be noted over the entire planet. While it was thought at first in other cities that the shock meant simply that an unidentified earthquake had occurred somewhere, the worldwide effects were more startling. Apparently the magnetic field of the earth was affected. Magnets behaved erratically in different cities all at the exact moment of the Tunguska explosion. Horses were seen to lose their balance in locations as far away as San Francisco, New York, and cities in Europe. Atmospheric pressure fluctuated violently at points thousands of miles apart. For several days afterward a strong orange glow lit up the night skies over northern Europe; there are records of telephone enquiries in England as to whether London was on fire.

Nevertheless it took the rest of the world over twenty years to realize that something quite different from an earthquake had occurred. As John Baxter and Thomas Atkins point out in their study of the explosion *(The Fire Came By:* 1976) the incident was not properly investigated at the time because of the isolation of the locale and the intervening preoccupation of Russia with war and revolution. Only many years later came the dawning realization, in the words of scientist Felix Zigel, "We do not know but what on June 30, 1908, the earth collided with some extraordinary, still unfamiliar, but natural heavenly body." Other scientists were later to express opinions still farther afield.

The Siberian peasants who experienced the blast, were doubtless influenced by their own religion's prophecies of doom and predictions of the world's end, and reacted to the manifestation with prayer and lamentations, convinced that the fateful day had indeed arrived. They had seen a "fiery pillar" in the heavens, the sky was rent by a white blast of light, forests burst into flame and whole herds of reindeer disappeared as if by magic. A cannonading of thunder deafened the terrified people within the extensive area, shocks threw them to the ground, and fierce winds blew away their houses and possessions even as they prayed for forgiveness and protection. The Tungus tribesmen, however, somewhat more pragmatically, simply ascribed the event to Ogdy, the Fire God, and thereupon quit the area and continued to give it a wide berth and preferred, in the hope of future forbearance on the part of Ogdy, not even to mention it.

Russian scientific interest began to develop after the long and disastrous civil wars that followed World War I. The area of the Tunguska "comet" or meteorite was finally reached and investigated in 1927 by Leonid Kulick, a researcher of meteorites, primarily in the hope of locating a great iron core under the frozen ground. But no core was found and no crater was found either; nothing but a destroyed forest with broken and burned trees, some standing stripped of their branches at the apparent blast center or what we would call at a later age "point zero," while others lay in great circular formations pointing away from the central blast.

It is interesting to reflect that witnesses and researchers of the Tunguska event interpreted it in terms of concepts with which they were familiar: the Siberian peasants with the end of the world, the Tungus tribesmen with the anger of the Fire God, and Russian scientists with comets or meteorites. However, some time after new knowledge of matter and thermonuclear reactions had burst upon the world in 1945 at Alamogordo, Hiroshima, and Nagasaki, it began to occur to some Soviet scientists that there was possibly another explanation of an atmospheric explosion close to the surface of the earth, an explosion whose force was later estimated at 30 megatons—1,500 times the power of the atom bomb dropped on Hiroshima. The descriptions by witnesses of some of the results of the 1908 blast parallel future events that would become distressingly familiar to everyone thirty-seven years later. They told of a flash of incredible brightness and a mushrooming black cloud, the seering heat of a thermal blast, the pressure of a shock wave, the sudden winds and fire storm, the falling of black rain, and the contamination of the skin and forming of scabs on the surviving reindeer. More than twenty-five years later the area proved to be surprisingly radioactive with a resultant change in plant growth.

Alexander Kazentsev, a Soviet space researcher, with several other astrophysicists, formed the opinion that the meteorite was actually a spacecraft which exploded in a thermonuclear reaction because of the melting of its protective covering as it entered the earth's atmosphere, and the resultant chain reaction explosion of its atomic plant. In his theory, the occupants of the spacecraft were probably attempting to get water, presumably from Lake Baikal, the largest and deepest (one mile) collection of freshwater in Eurasia. By piecing together accounts of varied witnesses who had observed the object in flight over a trajectory of almost a thousand miles a "flight" pattern has even been established. The object approached from the southwest, then turning and changing its approach to west it seemed to be maneuvering for a landing it was never to make.

Presuming the spacecraft to have been friendly and that perhaps it was purposely avoiding populated centers, Frank Edwards, an American commentator on scientific anomalies, observed in *Stranger than Science* (1959): "In the catastrophe along the Yenisei River in 1908 we lost a guest from the Universe."

Until a core or a crater is found it will not be known what actually caused the Tunguska explosion. A recent (February 1980) announcement from the *Sotsialisticheskaya Industria* of Moscow has stated that it was definitely a meteor since tiny carbonaro diamonds had been discovered in the Vanavara explosion area. These small diamonds are thought to be produced by the compression impact of the collision of celestial bodies, in this case the Encke comet which sends small meteor showers to Earth each year. This "final" explanation, perhaps stemming from an understandable uneasiness regarding unidentified thermonuclear activity over the U.S.S.R., is nevertheless double edged since thousands of small lustrous grains have been found for years in the Tunguska area and these grains are similar to the trinitite particles found at the atomic testing site at Alamogordo.

But whether the Tunguska incident was caused by a giant meteorite, a comet or part of a comet, or an alien space craft, the multimegaton blast if it took place today over a large metropolitan area of the globe, would kill millions and probably cause a retaliatory strike by one of the nuclear powers which would in turn precipitate a worldwide Doomsday.

Although the theory of black holes in space had not

yet been promulgated by scientists at the time of the incident or later, during the investigation, the possibility of the encounter of the earth with one of the universe's black holes has now been suggested as a cause of the enormous explosion.

These sinister sounding areas are thought to be a previously unsuspected state of matter, caused by the flaring up and subsequent implosion and collapse of dying stars as they burn out, to a state of density from which not even light can escape and which attracts and "swallows" all other matter which comes within its area of attraction. According to some astronomical theory the universe may contain hundreds of millions of black holes of all sizes—impossible exactly to estimate since they cannot be seen.

Walter Sullivan, science editor of the New York *Times* considers the possibility in his book *Black Holes* (1979) that a small black hole came into contact with the earth in the area of the stony Tunguska River in 1908 and caused the tremendous impact whose results can still be seen. It may then have *passed through* the earth increasing in size as it captured more matter and perhaps existing through the bottom of the Atlantic Ocean. The shock of leaving the planet through the sea would probably have been noted as a seaquake occurring in a midocean area where such temblors are common, especially in the Atlantic Ridge. The black hole would then continue out into space where, as is considered to be the case with other black holes, it would continue to grow as it constantly engorged more matter, gases, planetoids, planets, suns, and eventually whole solar systems, all of which would become part of the ever-growing black hole. Although it is some consolation to remember that the presence of large or small black holes is still a theory, it is a theory, nevertheless, that is sustained by a growing number of astronomers and one that has seemingly knocked out the floor from under the comfortable observatory from which we contemplate the universe. If the earth, in its meanderings through space, came within the "encounter horizon" of such a large black hole, the earth, the sun, and virtually everything in the solar system, could theoretically be drawn into it, compressed to the size of a pea and lost within an eternity of inky blackness.

Fortunately, the purported black holes that astrophysicists think they have identified within our galaxy are far from our solar system and do not seem (yet) to be approaching it. And even if one were, there would be time for scientists to identify it and for the earth's governments to consider mass immigration to another area of the cosmos, a rather cogent argument for the exploration of space while there is still time.

The theory of black holes is based upon astronomical observations that seem to have no other explanation. Radio signals from stars seem to bend around dark areas that, although they cannot be seen, must necessarily be there. The same happens with certain stars which seem occasionally to be pulled off their orbits by powerful forces which should be stars but which give no light. Gases and matter spinning off stars into space are attracted into areas where they disappear into the darkness of the black holes which may represent a process which will eventually swallow up the universe—either signifying an end or a new phase within or on the other side of the black holes.

One wonders whether the present day astronomers are the first to have noted the menace that the black hole theory implies. Walter Sullivan, in observing that many astrophysicists consider that Cygnus X-1* in our galaxy may be an example of a black hole, makes

---

* The invisible Cygnus X-1 is considered to be a black hole because the Uhuru satellite detected a tremendous energy volume of X-rays coming from the *vicinity* of, but not directly from, a massive star in the constellation Cygnus. The visible star, on an erratic orbit—as if something were pulling it off course—was obviously being affected by an invisible object (if we can call a black hole an object) with a tremendous gravitational pull, in other words a suspected black hole.

mention of a startling coincidence. The ancient Sumerians, precursers of the Babylonians, Assyrians, and other early astronomers, identified this same area as the abode of the "Demon Bird" of the god Nergal, Lord of the Underworld, and as an area of death and darkness. If, as it has been suggested, some of the very early cultures were descending and not ascending the ladder of civilization, then someone more than 6,000 years ago, through means doubtless different from those of modern astronomy but nevertheless effective, had observed the flare-up of a dying sun and its disappearance into darkness, and had labeled that area of the sky as a place of danger, which it may, if the theory is correct, eventually prove to be.

One remembers, however, that the black hole theory is based on the theoretical observations of many of the same scientists who pioneered work on the atom bomb, including Oppenheimer, Einstein, Fermi, Teller, Wigner, Von Neumann, Weblen, and others. The atom bomb was a theory too, until the bomb was successfully exploded, whereupon it became an actuality. That event subsequently affected the outlook and the lives of all the dwellers on this planet.

Although an encounter between Earth and a wandering black hole appears remote at the present time, there are other less spectacular potentialities which are no less dangerous and more probable, because they have happened before. One, for example, would be a drop in the earth's climate caused by passing through cosmic dust clouds in space, affecting the earth's atmosphere and the strength of the sun's heat rays as received on Earth. Our planet together with the sun and the other planets, moons and asteroids, makes a round trip around the galaxy approximately every 200 million years. Our location, in regard to the middle of the Milky Way galaxy, is about two-thirds away from the galactic center toward its spiral arms. As the earth makes its great circling trip we pass in and out of these spiral arms, and it is within these arms that we pass through great quantities of cosmic dust, while the areas between the arms are relatively dust free. It is calculated that we are within one of these dust-laden areas at the present time, at the edge of the Orion spiral arm, with the possibility that our weather is even now being affected by a change in our normal climate, a supposition that seems fairly possible in view of the climatic variations of the past few years.

But should this 200-million-year long trip of our solar system cause us any concern at present, before we mentally file it away as an interesting fact? *If* the earth is getting colder, the answer is yes—even a small deviation in our weather pattern toward colder winters, and the obvious connection with oil shortages, will bring on not only physical but also social and political problems, which we are observing at this very moment.

As for the possibility of a new Ice Age now starting, we have some interesting indications. There is the enormous increase of ice in Antarctica (five million square miles of it, up to three miles thick), the widening of the ice cap in the Arctic, the cooling of the North Atlantic, the intensity and lengthening of winters during the past few years and, somewhat more ominously, the fact that glaciers in the northern hemisphere—retreating until 1940—stopped their retreat and began once more to advance. Also, if the seismic and volcanic disturbances occur as predicted in the next decade, the resultant volcanic dust will increase the effect of cosmic dust by cutting down even more the warming effect of the sun.

During the last Ice Age, glacial ice covered 30 percent of all land areas. We can easily foresee the catastrophic results that would be caused in the world's already short food supply, dependent on normal climate, by rapid cooling, even before the future glaciers came. And finally, there appears to be a ten thousand year interval between glacial periods, with fluctuations of short cold periods toward the end of an intervening warm era, that serves to announce the approaching era of cold. Perhaps the relatively recent cold period (sometimes called "the little ice age"), which occurred in the late seventeenth and early eighteenth centuries, was just such an announcement.

There is yet another cosmic danger to Earth's population that might happen unpredictably and is thought to have happened before in the earth's long and perilous history. This concerns radiation from space, strong enough to pass through the magnetic shield with disastrous effects on living beings. Ordinarily, the magnetic field of the earth (generated it is thought by Earth's inner currents and its rotation), coupled with our atmosphere, are strong enough to protect the earth from outer space radiation. This protection, however, may be weakened during certain periods of magnetic reversal when the field weakens and allows more charged radiation to pass through it. A special source of radiation would be a nova flare-up while the earth, on its journey through space, was near enough to the burst to be affected.

We cannot at present know when a dying star might suddenly burst into a nova. It has been calculated, however, that a supernova strong enough to affect this planet would occur perhaps within the space of every fifty million years. The disappearance of dinosaurs took place approximately sixty-five million years ago. The reversal of the magnetic field and/or the radiation from a supernova or an abnormally large solar flare have been explored to explain one of the earth's great mysteries, the sudden collective death of the dinosaurs at the end of the Mesozoic era after having lived on the earth for 140 million years. But not only the dinosaurs were affected; 70 percent of all animal species vanished and 50 percent of all Earth's plants at the same time. Proportions of disappearances in a previous mass holocaust at the end of the Permian period were even higher, although they have been less commented on since the Permian disappearances happened 230 million years ago, while the more recent and dramatic dinosaur disappearance (65 million years before present) remains a favorite subject for popular conjecture.

Theories concerning the sudden and mysterious end of the dinosaurs include the following: The dinosaurs disappeared because they could not survive one of the early ice ages or even a relatively cold period; the surface waters of the earth decreased and reduced their feeding area; an emerging and increasing animal population at the end of the Cretaceous era developed

There is an intriguing possibility that some reptiles of the tertiary period may have survived the dinosaur extinction and still be alive in the abysses of the sea. The most frequent descriptions of such creatures as reported by DSRVs (deep sea research vehicles) seem to tally with reconstruction of the plesiosaurus, which supposedly vanished with the dinosaurs at the time of the Cretaceous extinction. It has been suggested that deep inland lakes such as Loch Ness may contain other such survivors who adapted to changed conditions.

a fatal (to the dinosaurs) fondness for dinosaur eggs; dinosaurs ran out of living space suitable to their needs because of a change in Earth's climate; a supernova exploded relatively close to the earth, killing off the dinosaurs through radiation; or a reversal or intermission of Earth's magnetic field exposed them to cosmic radiation, either killing them outright or causing such genetic mutations that they effectively disappeared as dinosaurs.

One somewhat startling interpretation of the last theory is that dinosaurs have not disappeared at all and that they still live on in their considerably modified direct descendants, the birds. And, if some sea-going dinosaurs had adapted to deep water they might have escaped the cosmic radiation that would have destroyed the species on the earth's land and shallow water areas. In this case it is conceivable that some of them still exist in the abyssal depths of the ocean and have given rise to the legends of sea serpents so often and insistently reported by past and present seamen, ships' passengers, and sea captains. Captain McCamis of the DSRV *Alvin* (deep submergence research vessel) encountered a monster later identified as a plesiosaurus on a deep dive within the Bahamas, a prehistoric survivor identical in appearance with descriptions of the Loch Ness monster within the preglacial Great Glen of Scotland.

One remembers, with regard to prehistoric sea survivals, that the coelacanth, a large fossil fish with "legs" (supposedly extinct for twenty million years) was taken alive in the Indian Ocean near Madagascar in 1938 and that several more were netted shortly thereafter.

Recently (1980) another variation of the theory regarding the cosmic radiation death of the dinosaurs has been proposed by Dr. Luis W. Alvarez, a Nobel laureate in physics of the Lawrence Berkeley Laboratory in California, which suggests that the earth was struck by a giant meteorite 65 million years ago—the time of the

Great Dying. His theory is based on the finding of an iridium layer (iridium is created by solar flare and supernova explosions) in rock layers dated after the dinosaur era and supposes that the cosmic dust from the explosion, blocking off the sunlight, disrupted the food chain and caused the death of the species by eventual starvation. This is especially provocative since it implies that a meteor several miles in diameter could strike the earth suddenly, or that an enormous volcanic explosion could occur, causing such final effects to a species through interrupting the food sup-

Although the coelacanth, a fish with certain land-animal attributes such as partially developed limbs and a vestigial lung, lived during the Mesozoic era at least sixty million years ago, several live specimens were taken by fishermen in the Indian Ocean near the African coast just before World War II. This unusual example of a creature whose development was arrested and who survived through millions of years brings up the possibility that there may exist other survivals of Mesozoic fauna which, by living in the sea, escaped the cosmic rays which, according to one theory, may have caused the dinosaur extinction.

ply, even without considering the destructive and other effects of the cosmic rays from space.

The mass disappearance of the giant saurians from the earth may have been due to a combination of factors, most importantly perhaps to a magnetic reversal of the planet's poles. During the time of such a magnetic reversal the magnetic field weakens and therefore, during such a magnetic "intermission" the earth would be more vulnerable to strikes by meteors and comets as well as exposures to cosmic rays. Dr. Ian Crane of the Australian National University, as quoted by Fred Warshofsky, a scientist and author (*Doomsday, the Science of Catastrophe:* 1977) has declared:

Mass extinctions are caused directly by the deleterious effects on organisms of the reduced magnetic field during a reversal.

In the opinion of Dr. Manson Valentine, author and zoologist:

The sudden appearance of a new animal kingdom after the dinosaur's extinction was caused by genetic changes brought on by the magnetic reversal. At the end of the Mesozoic era not primitive but modern specialized reptiles, modern birds, modern insects, and modern mammals all arrived at the same time as if by sudden metamorphosis. Diatoms suddenly covered the sea and modern plants appeared as if summoned by a new creational force. Evolution did not proceed gradually but evolved suddenly at the time of a basic magnetic flux.

One wonders which, if any, of the earth's species will vanish during the next magnetic reversal. According to the incidence of magnetic reversals in the past another major magnetic reversal should have occurred long before now. It has been noted by some scientists that there seems to be a reduction in the intensity of the earth's magnetic field, an indication of the start of a new reversal which hopefully will come far enough in the future to give us time to devise sufficient protection against radiation from outer space.

Whether our protective magnetic field increases or decreases is something we are presently unable to control. But there is another protective shield that we may even now be in the process of destroying.

Within the cosmos there seems to exist a delicate balance between benefit and danger—a truism equally applicable to life itself. The earth, for example, has a further protective shield, the ozone layer, which exists high in the earth's atmosphere and to which we owe our continued existence. This ozone layer is a field of ionization which, in effect, maintains a transparent wall between Earth's upper atmosphere and the sun, permitting us to benefit from the life-giving heat and light of the sun and protecting us at the same time from the sun's ultraviolet radiation. For, without this ozone shield, this same life-giving force, the sun, would destroy the life it is sustaining.

This protective screen is being increasingly damaged by the wide use of gaseous fluorocarbon (Freon) operated spray cans of pesticides, fertilizers, beauty aids, antiseptics, household cleaners, and the exhausts of supersonic jets as they pass through the ozone layer.

We have an example of outstanding paradox in the actions of suntan spray users who, while enjoying the sun on a pleasant beach, inadvertently contribute to

On facing page, chart of the principal earth time divisions in the life of Earth dwellers, the areas indicated to the left and the periods on the right. Marked changes in animal life such as the disappearance of dinosaurs have occurred rather suddenly at different periods, possibly caused by magnetic radiation or long interference by circling cosmic dust with the light of the sun. From a point of view of cosmic catastrophe, today's regnant inhabitants of the Earth would, one hopes, find a way to avoid the fate of the dinosaurs.

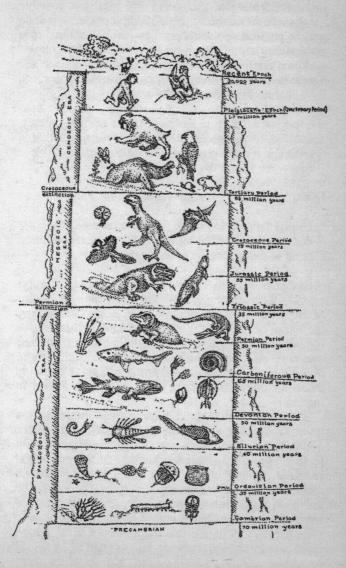

Recent Epoch
30,000 years

Pleistocene Epoch (Quaternary Period)
1.7 million years

CENOZOIC ERA

Cretaceous
extinction

Tertiary Period
65 million years

MESOZOIC ERA

Cretaceous Period
75 million years

Jurassic Period
55 million years

Permian
extinction

Triassic Period
35 million years

Permian Period
50 million years

PALEOZOIC ERA

Carboniferous Period
65 million years

Devonian Period
50 million years

Silurian Period
40 million years

Ordovician Period
35 million years

Cambrian Period
70 million years

PRECAMBRIAN

the deterioration of the shield that makes it possible for them to sit on the beach in the first place. Someone with a passion for statistics has estimated that, in a normal day's sunbathing on the Riviera, fifty couples spraying each other with tanning lotion damage the ozone layer the equivalent of one supersonic contrail for one day. Fred Warshofsky states:

> Some estimates claim that the Freon already released will reduce the ozone shield from 3 to 6%. A 5% reduction is estimated to cause 8,000 new cases of skin cancer per year in the United States. . . .

In contemplating a further reduction he adds:

> Ultraviolet radiation would become so intense it would destroy crops in the fields and alter the weather to the point where agriculture would be threatened. . . .

Statistics such as these, however alarming, are frequently forgotten by people intent on the advantages of superjet travel, household aids, convenience, and industrial protection. While this gradual weakening of the ozone shield will no doubt be more widely realized and corrective measures taken, there is another more definite peril that comes, like other dangers awaiting us in an uncertain future, from a miscalculation in nuclear warfare.

A nuclear bomb could blow a hole in the ozone layer. This hole, according to the size of the bomb, could leave a prolonged gap over a target area, subjecting the enemy targets beneath it to prolonged radiation from the sun. This could happen through explosions of nuclear bombs at certain levels over the earth—it might be attempted as a preventive strike or even as a warning. But it would seem to be obvious to scientists of any nation that a hole blown in the ozone layer would have worldwide effects caused by winds or erratic behavior of the hole. Nevertheless there might be nations or groups which would take the chance of such a nuclear action to attain their aims.

It would appear that the more we advance scientifically the closer we come to the possibility of our own destruction as a species as well as that of the pleasant world on which we live.

6

Pandora's Box

The ancient Greek legend of Pandora and the locked coffer which she could not resist opening is one of the most persistent and perennially applicable of myths. Pandora, according to legend, was created by Hephaestus, out of earth as a revenge by the gods on human beings for the gift of fire they had received from Prometheus. Each of the gods gave her a special power. She was given supreme beauty and seductive powers by Aphrodite, the goddess of beauty, and the art of flattery and cunning by the god Hermes, and so on. Pandora then became the bride of Epimetheus, the simple-minded brother of Prometheus, who had stolen the divine secret of fire from the gods on Mount Olympus. Prometheus, fearing revenge from Zeus, the father of the gods, was determined to avoid further contact including the acceptance of gifts. He warned his brother Epimetheus that Zeus would probably soon be about some divine trickery and so it was: Zeus gave a beautiful closed jar (later translated as "box") to the married couple with special instructions that it not be opened. But Pandora, admiring the jar and thinking that it probably contained more godly knowledge or gifts equivalent to the use of fire, could not refrain from secretly opening it, with the results that we all know. What she thought would be of benefit resulted in a plague of diseases and disasters which flew out of the jar and quickly spread over the world.

In a modern application of Pandora's box it would appear that much of our scientific, medical, and above all military development in recent years, although undoubtedly progress, may have an end result quite different from the Utopia for which such progress was directed. Forces have been unleashed by modern technology whose dangerous and perhaps final effects have just begun to be realized. Certain self-destructive trends, unless interrupted and reversed, appear to indicate a crisis of civilization within the next two decades, caused by population pressure. In other words, by the end of the second millennium, there may be a crisis at first view less dramatic than the predicted astronomical dangers, but apparently more certain unless something can be done to avoid it.

According to controlled estimates the world population is now doubling every thirty-seven years although in past centuries the doubling of the population occurred on a descending scale of from ten thousand to one thousand years. At the present time, despite wars and widespread starvation, the rate of increase is growing in geometric progression: one billion in 1830, two billion by 1930, three billion by 1960, and approaching five billion in 1980.

As the population grows starvation increases. Even the scientific improvements in agriculture such as techniques developed by the "Green Revolution" program exported worldwide by the United States, has failed to alleviate hunger in that its results have substantially increased the population in countries already overpopulated. More than five million people die of starvation every year, mostly in the Third World where more than 40 percent of the population is under fifteen years of age. One can imagine the increasing pressure in living space, the struggle for food and employment, and the transportation breakdown in some of the world's cities which act as a magnet for the surrounding depressed areas. To give an example it has been calculated that if the present trend continues the population of Calcutta will increase to sixty-five or seventy million inhabitants by the year 2000. It is interesting to note that Lenin, in one of his frequent pronouncements, once said that the final breakdown of capitalism would start in some colonially developed city of Asia, specifically naming Calcutta as a possibility. This is only one example among many cities where the population is tending to exceed housing, transportation, and food supply on a vertiginous careen to an eventual complete breakdown.

If world population is not modified soon the earth will be filled with so many people that they and their dwellings will cover the whole habitable planet, even over the deserts and sides of mountains and extending on specially built platforms out to sea. Robert Silverberg, who in a science fiction novel which is really a treatise on the future (*The World Inside:* 1974) presents a not illogical picture of future developments as he describes monstrous dwellings hundreds of stories high and extending deep into the ground, with small artificial green belts in between, which the inhabitants may only view from their vast warrens but not enter.

There will be no free land anywhere, forests and parks will be gone; the food problems that today are difficult will become insoluble; mineral and fuel resources will be exhausted (all petroleum sources, that is, the estimated 660 billion barrels still unpumped, will be exhausted by 2017 or sooner if the present rate of consumption increases); water will be in short supply; all the wild animals and most domestic ones will have disappeared. All this will doubtlessly be aggravated by upheavals, revolutions, and perhaps more wars as the have-not nations become unwilling to wait for wider participation in the sharing of the world's resources.

But even if there is no widespread breakdown and if

the world population continues to increase at a rate of geometric progression, we may soon reach a "heat limit" where the heat generated by the living of these enormous future multitudes and from their heat-producing cities will affect the climate, as it has already begun to do. As the fields and trees vanish the various human activities, including even breathing, will tend to produce still more carbon dioxide, further warming the earth's atmospheric envelope and increasing the "greenhouse" effect which will keep the earth's heat from dissipating into space. This tendency has already been hastened by the burning of fossil fuels which has increased the carbon dioxide in the atmosphere 30 percent within the present century. A comparatively slight warming of the earth's climate, even four degrees, will produce melting of the arctic ice with attendant flooding of large sections of the earth just as was prophesied for this time period centuries before the greenhouse effect and its consequences were ever thought of.

While it is possible that the earth is growing colder in a normal progression of warm and cold periods, a runaway greenhouse effect could reverse such a cooling tendency with catastrophic results for the world at large since the affected areas would be where population and industry are most concentrated. In addition, such a heat increase would affect crops all over the world, adding starvation to the worldwide disaster.

When population, human or animal, gets out of control something uaually happens to bring down the numbers. In nature boundless increase of animal population is limited in a variety of ways. Sometimes species are decimated by starvation or more generally kept within bounds by cropping by predators such as wolves, lions, and other carnivores which prey on both animal herds and on smaller mammals; birds whose feeding acts as a break on the number of insects; and cats which instinctively control the explosive rodent population. Isaac Asimov points out in his recent book (*A Choice of Catastrophes:* 1979) that a female rat, giving birth to sixty young every year would, as its progeny also followed this procreational cycle, within seventy years have spawned a rat population whose combined weight would be greater than that of the earth itself. Fortunately this has not happened, nor is it likely to, partially because of human control but principally because rats suffer sudden diseases or plagues at times. Sometimes, as in the case of the Black Death of the fourteenth century, a rat-carried disease has attacked human beings. The Black Death, brought by rats in ships from Asia to Europe, devastated cities, the countryside, and whole nations, killing perhaps a third of the population of Europe and Asia and convincing those that had not yet died that the end of the world was effectively at hand.

In other cases overnumerous animal populations unconsciously control their numbers by mass suicide. The rodent lemmings of Scandinavia, upon reaching a certain population density, swarm into the North Atlantic Ocean in great mass waves, swimming westward until they drown. (This phenomenon has often been cited as an inherited race memory of a fertile land that once existed between Europe and North America. But, whether or not the lemmings possess an inherited memory, the population control by suicide is still effective.)

Limitations to the growth of Earth's human population have been removed fairly recently by technology and developments in medicine. Everyone now alive in the United States has a chance of living considerably longer than if he or she had been born one hundred or even fifty years earlier. This, coupled with a decrease in infant mortality, has increased the population pressure to a degree no longer compatible with Earth's space and resources. Before mankind developed his present means to conquer and exploit nature and to preserve and increase his own species, the overpopulation problem in a particular area was often solved by immigration to new areas as well as by warfare, plagues, and natural or man-made disasters.

Today the "emigration solution" is becoming increasingly difficult. The "final solution" of overpopulation by warfare, however, is a possibility evident to anyone who reads the press or listens to the evening news. Another possibility is the reduction in numbers by the appearance of a new disease virus similar to the then "untreatable" plagues of the Middle Ages. Such a visitation might develop by itself or a virus created for biological warfare might "escape" even in peacetime, and propagate itself worldwide. Unlike the former slower progress of virulent disease transported by ships or invading tribes or armies, it could spread almost immediately over the earth via the thousands of daily passenger air flights.

A new disease, or plague, might even come from the cosmos itself, either from a strain present in the cosmic dust clouds through which our solar system frequently passes, or unwittingly brought back to earth by our astronauts (one remembers the long decontamination process after the first landing) from future landings on planets or planetary moons.

Still another possibility is a reduction in our numbers through misuse of technology. Although we have little control over natural disasters we are, as a species and often individually, responsible for man-made ones and like the lemmings of Scandinavia who breed and eat themselves out of existence, must face the results if we run out of living space and raw materials of all kinds. Not-so-early warning signals have already been given.

Croplands have been poisoned by toxic chemicals; crucial wetlands are being filled in for housing; the air over some of the earth's cities is dangerous to breathe; woodlands are being cleared for housing and industry or destroyed by stripmining; and rivers, lakes, and even the ocean have become increasingly polluted by chemical wastes. Even the great tropical rain forests have already been half destroyed, and the remaining half is being demolished at the rate of fifty acres every minute as the countries of the Third World open areas for settlement and industry.

Many of the world's rivers have become so over-charged with refuse that they have been described as "too thin to plow and too thick to drink" as they continue to carry their dangerous chemicals into the sea. The vast amounts of pollutants entering the ocean, more than half a million noxious substances, are poisoning marine life and perhaps, through the poisoning of the basic marine diatoms which absorb carbon dioxide and produce oxygen, may eventually make the atmosphere of the earth unbreathable.

The ancient legend of Pandora's box needs only a change of view to become as applicable today as it was in the time of the gods. The present-day Box of Pandora contains the potential of modern technology which, if released too quickly and without control, as it has been up to now, will produce a self-induced disaster.

One such technical "improvement" was the indis-criminate use of DDT for crop dusting and insect control which later proved to have dangerous future residual effects for the human beings it was meant to protect as well as for the pests it was intended to eliminate. Dr. Manson Valentine, then a biologist in-volved in early DDT testing for the Department of Agriculture in Washington, was a witness to its lethal force. The experiment took place in 1948. Dr. Valen-tine remembers:

I was on call in the National Museum, Washington, to identify the species of insects, in my case beetles and butterflies, which were exterminated by spraying DDT from planes in a selected test area. The area chosen was a tract of 1000 acres, most of the only virgin forest left in Maryland, along the bank of the Potomac above

Chain Bridge. The purpose of the project was to find out what DDT would kill and how long it would take.

The result was that there was no life left at all.

Everything was killed from protozoa to mammals. Everything that flew, climbed, scampered, burrowed, or swam was sent in enormous quantities to a large group of biologists. We had to make long reports on each species, hundreds of species with thousands of members of each.

It turned out it was fatal to humans too. As a side effect of the experiment the gardener who worked for a colleague of mine, Dr. Paul Bartsch, a specialist in mollusks, died as a result of the DDT he was using in Dr. Bartsch's garden.

As I was working on the experiment I began to have "end of the world" thoughts. It occurred to me that if the unrestrained use of DDT were spread it would kill off the animal population and eventually people as well. Fortunately for the rest of us other human fatalities began to occur and the use of DDT was interrupted in the United States after some years. However, it is still used in Central and South America where entire species of insects, birds, and small animals continue to disappear.

Considering the subsequent use of DDT and other insecticides throughout the world one realizes that the fatal effects on insects, birds, and animals in the same food chain that humans use may have been understood too late. The effects of DDT are now being noted far from its original point of use.

It has been ascertained that DDT builds up at the top of the food chain, namely the carnivores, the group of which we form a part. Within the body tissue of Americans the DDT rate now stands at 11 ppm (parts per million) and other tested groups, such as the Israelis, show even higher rates—19.2 ppm. The Eskimos and the fish-eating seals in the cold waters of the

Arctic show between 23 and 25 ppm and even the seals and penguins of the Antarctic show high concentrations although living at Earth's farthest point from DDT treated areas.

Although the use of DDT has been interrupted in the U.S. (but still widely used elsewhere), thousands of comparable chemical compound incidents have taken place and are still happening. They all relate to immediate and cumulative dangers created by human decisions. They vary in type but are generally connected by a central theme: profit and convenience now and disregard for or ignorance of the consequences.

While recent developments at Three Mile Island have captured the public imagination, a selection of some other less publicized happenings are indicative of man-made poisoning of the air, land, and sea.

- The great soft-coal fogs which formed over London in the fifties are calculated to have killed thousands of persons. At the time it was pointed out that most of these victims suffered from respiratory diseases or were simply old and would have died anyhow. However, the enormous increase in the daily death rates suggests that most of the people died as a result of the smoky fogs, as is more obviously the case with the death fogs in coal mining regions. Nowadays the smogs over Tokyo, Los Angeles, Mexico City, and other areas are caused mainly by gasoline fumes, which become more lethal during inversion periods. The industrial and gasoline smogs over the Ruhr in Germany sometimes blow over the North Sea and cover areas over southern England, a presage of what would happen during nuclear warfare when the dangerous nuclear clouds might travel to non-participating countries.
- On November 10, 1979, as a result of a derailment of tank cars, a propane explosion in one car caused a leak in another car carrying ninety tons of chlo-

rine gas, enough to wipe out the population of a whole city. Immediate action by the authorities evacuated 250,000 persons from Missisauga, Ontario, until the chlorine was secured.

- In Iraq, 1972, grain seed treated with methyl mercury was distributed to the people of a large village. The farmers used it to feed their animals and also for baking bread. The subsequent death toll was 459 and over 6,500 people became seriously ill.

- The Love Canal, an old, abandoned canal at Niagara Falls had long been used (1942-53) by the Hooker Chemical and Plastics Corporation as a dump for industrial wastes comprising an estimated eighty to one hundred varieties of toxic chemical materials which were covered over and buried. Subsequently family housing and even an elementary school were built on the site. It was eventually noticed that approximately 50 percent of all children living from birth in houses built over the fill possessed or developed some sort of defect in their vital organs, nerves or limbs, and there were even cases where they grew three sets of teeth. These chromosomal defects had developed, presumably, from genetic deficiencies in their parents caused by their living environment.

  Documentation of a high miscarriage rate and the observed bubbling up of buried chemicals to the surface prompted the New York State government to evacuate and relocate families from houses within the first two construction rings over the center of the former dump area. The two rings were then closed off behind a wire fence. In 1980, however, renewed testing and indications of genetic and chromosome damage brought the matter up again and it was found that a more extensive contiguous area seemed to be affected. Additional residents demanded to be moved out at government expense and to be reimbursed for 'their property. (The issue has been complicated by a state claim that part of the waste material buried in the canal originated from the Manhattan Project—radium, uranium, and other radioactive materials left over from the development of the original atomic bomb.)

What is especially disturbing about this incident is that apparently the first relocations in 1978 were not sufficient and that the extent of expanding danger beneath the ground was finally determined only by the effect on the people living there. On a larger scale, no one can know—until the effects on what one might call the human guinea pigs are noted—how many hundreds or thousands of potentially dangerous areas exist throughout the industrial world.

• In Minamata, Japan, where the people subsist mainly on fish, it became apparent that inordinate numbers of the villagers were dying, suffering from brain and nerve damage, and that newborn babies had symptoms of cerebral palsy. Medical research verified that they had been ingesting methyl mercury dumped from a nearby factory, swallowed by fish, and finally absorbed into the bodies of the fish-eating villagers. In Northern Japan hundreds of cases of sickness and many deaths occurred over a period of twelve years, starting in 1955 as a result of cadmium poisoning, traceable to the rice and soy beans grown in fields close to industries that use cadmium in their processes. This new disease, which is extremely painful, affecting the joints and robbing the bones of calcium, was named by the words most frequently uttered by the victims, *Itai-itai* ("It hurts, it hurts").

• The Great Lakes, which contain 95 percent of all the fresh water in the forty-eight continental states of the United States, are polluted by more than four hundred chemical compounds. Asbestos, a cause of cancer, has been identified even in Lake Superior, the most northern of the Great Lakes, which is used as a source of drinking water. Some of the rivers that empty into the lakes are so affected that in the case of the Cuyahoga River, which runs into Lake Erie, the water itself caught fire on two occasions, and the Detroit River at one point became so noxious that its waters were able to eat through metal.

- Even the open ocean has been seriously polluted in various places near the great ports. Twenty-five miles southwest of New York City a large area devoid of fish life has formed where sludge has been dumped off the coast of New Jersey. The dead area is increasing as it moves toward the Jersey shore and also toward Long Island. Ocean beaches have frequently been closed during the summer to guard against disease threatened by the expanding sludge area. The dumping of industrial and other wastes has polluted the Mediterranean, reduced its fish population, and caused outbreaks of disease and death among those eating its seafood. As pollution increases, black warning flags and police periodically keep swimmers away from the formerly clear waters off the beaches of southern France and several other nations bordering on the Mediterranean.

- While the dangers of acid rain was the subject of mention by President Carter in his message to Congress in August, 1979, it had been evident for some time previously. The rainfall in the industrial countries consistently precipitates more acid as it falls on the earth. While all fossil fuel contributes to the constant acidic showers, coal, the use of which is increasing because of the oil impasse, is the main agent responsible for the ascent of nitrogen oxide and sulphur dioxide into the atmosphere and its descent as acid. As Kenneth Brower writes in an article *(Omni:* 1979):

Scientists of the International Joint Commission predict that, by 1995, 50,000 lakes in this country and Canada will be biologically dead; widespread destruction of plant and animal life will have occurred; and millions of people will have been contaminated by lead, mercury, aluminum, and cadmium removed by acid from soil, rock, and water pipes . . .

• While oil spills from supertankers are fatal to seabirds and ruinous to beaches, the oil may not be the chief danger it is usually considered to be as it is, in effect, biodegradable and even digestible to some forms of marine life. If, however, a supertanker should disintegrate in the ice area of the Arctic or Antarctic it is possible that it could cause a self-perpetuating melting of the ice, triggering a worldwide flooding of coastal and low-lying areas.

• In 1970 the USS *Briggs,* a former Liberty Ship, was sunk by order of the U. S. Navy about 200 miles due east of the Georgia coast in waters about 15,000 feet deep. The reason: to get rid of a supply of stored nerve gas whose canisters were giving signs of erosion. Assurances were given by the Navy that the nerve gas would, if it escaped, be neutralized by dilution in sea water, a solution open to some doubt, as many substances, such as mercury, are not neutralized.

• The ocean will also probably be the recipient of the considerable amounts of atomic waste which is now being generated in the reactors of North America, Europe, and Asia and soon South America and Africa as well. It has been considered that the deep abysses of the ocean floor would hold this dangerous waste for generations although no one is sure. There are also suggestions that it somehow be conveyed out into space where its eventual orbiting of course would imperil not only Earth but the solar system and space as well.

- In the 1960s the U. S. Army tried dumping quantities of atomic waste from nuclear test sites into deep wells around Denver, Colorado. Shortly afterward hundreds of earthquakes occurred, many of which caused considerable damage in the Denver area, where earthquakes had seldom occurred in the past. Although denying any connection between the dumping and the temblors, the army authorities, under pressure from civilian law suits, stopped the underground waste disposal in the area and the earthquakes ceased.

- In 1968, years after the nuclear test explosion on Bikini, in the Marshall Islands, the evcuated natives were allowed to return. But when they began to farm the crops were found to be radioactive and the bewildered islanders were again evacuated. At Eniwetok, the nuclear blast site of 1947, the exiled population was permitted to vote on whether or not they wanted to return to the island which had undergone a radioactive waste cleanup. Coconut trees were planted for them to make up for the trees they had before, but the islanders were cautioned, in an injunction reminiscent of the Book of Genesis, that they were forbidden to eat the fruit (since the trees were grown in soil still presumed "hot" twenty years after the atomic bomb).

- Persistent rumors have been current in the U.S.S.R. and abroad since the middle of 1979 that biological warfare germs or a "lethal biological agent" stored at Soviet army facilities at or near Sverdlovsk U.S.S.R. (population one million) may have leaked into the city in April or May 1979, causing numerous fatalities. The resultant death toll in Sverdlovsk was reported at one thousand before the outbreak could be controlled. That the disease was a type of pulmonary anthrax is indicated by symptoms reported. The soldier casualties ran high fevers and their lips and ears turned blue. Autopsies showed that their lungs were filled with fluid. In March, 1980, United States Ambassador Thomas Watson delivered to the Soviet Union a demand for explanation concerning the violation of an international ban on "development, production, and stock-piling of microbiological agents or toxins."

• The ten million gallons of Agent Orange, the defoliant sprayed over the jungles of Vietnam, had a byproduct, dioxin, considered to be a million times more poisonous than some other chemical poisons such as PCB. Individual veterans are now preparing cases based on ill health caused by their exposure to the Agent Orange defoliant. Quantities of Agent Orange are still stored at Gulfport, Mississippi, and will eventually have to be dumped somewhere, no doubt into the ocean.

• While the nuclear disaster at Three Mile Island has caused a long look at the operation of nuclear plants in the United States, a recent Nuclear Regulatory Commission ruling has nevertheless stated that the accident, according to the Price Anderson Act limitations on accident liability, cannot be considered an "extraordinary nuclear occurence." Perhaps a good example of what definitely would be an "extraordinary nuclear occurence" in peacetime reputedly took place near Kyshtym, close to the Ural Mountains in the U.S.S.R. Kyshtym is an off-limits area not accessible to foreigners but which was, subsequent to the incident, visited by several Soviet scientists, some of whom have since defected. According to their reports, a spontaneous explosion of nuclear wastes at a plutonium processing plant, and resultant winds, had spread radioactive fallout over hundreds of square miles. Other theories place the blame on a faulty reactor or spillage caused by an earthquake. Although the incident was never officially admitted, there were reputedly thousands of casualties—killed, wounded, and sick, many from radiation sickness. A Russian physicist who traveled through the area several years later was quoted by *Time*, December 20, 1976, as describing the incident as follows:

> There were trees and grass but it was an empty land like the moon. There were no villages, no towns, only the chimneys of destroyed houses; no cultivated fields, no herds or people—nothing.

- Even controlled underground tests can have unexpected results. German and British seismologists believe that an underground thermonuclear test carried out in southern Siberia was instrumental in causing an earthquake near Tabas, Iran, on September 16, 1978. The earthquake occurred thirty-six hours after the nuclear explosion and killed 25,000 people in Iran.
- Experiments concerned with modifications of the earth and its natural forces, even for the best of reasons, have occasionally threatened catastrophes more serious than the conditions scientists were attempting to control. Dr. Gribbin, in *Earthquake*, describes a plan entertained by the government of Iceland, the U. S. Coast Guard, and the U. S. Navy to inhibit the lava flow of the Heimaey volcano in Iceland from blocking the port. An explosion was planned to break the lava crust and divert it from the Heimaey harbor. But those in charge of the experiment realized, before setting it in motion, that the fuel coolant "interaction" of the super-hot lava (2012° F.) mixing immediately with the cold seawater would produce an explosion, even under the planned charge, of a four-megaton bomb. The experiment was therefore aborted, happily for Iceland, which would

have been destroyed as the original explosion combined (as it would have) in a self-generating union with more hot lava and with seawater.

Never before in the history of man and his relationship with the earth has he been able so profoundly to modify his environment. Within a period of scarcely the last one hundred years his efforts, however, have produced some eminently unfavorable results to the remaining animal species he has not yet killed off, to humanity, and to the earth itself. John McHale, as quoted by G. Tylor Miller *(Living in the Environment: Concepts, Problems, and Alternatives: 1975)* has observed:

It is only in the most recent, and brief, period of his tenure that man has developed in sufficient numbers and acquired enough power, to become one of the most potentially dangerous organisms that the planet has ever hosted.

One wonders whether, to a cosmic observer, present-day man would be considered a benign or a malignant organism on the great living body which is the Earth.

Within the past years, however, some of the mistakes and reckless enthusiasm of progress at any cost have been subjected to more rigorous public scrutiny. Some of the more destructive tendencies have been curbed. The rivers and lakes of America have been undergoing periodic clean-ups after decades of abuse. The U. S. Department of Justice and the State of New York have both brought suit against the Hooker Chemical and Plastics Corporation (which used the now-famous Love Canal as a dump before it was closed in the 1950s), an action tending to initiate second thoughts among potential industrial polluters. Smog control is being implemented: London has ceased to burn soft coal and now enjoys clear weather. Pittsburgh has accomplished an unbelievable improvement in its weather and environment. The use of DDT has been curbed and the use of Freon, at least in the United States, was prohibited by law in 1979. Pesticides and chemical fertilizers are being carefully controlled. The disposal of atomic wastes and the security of nuclear reactor plants have become a matter of serious governmental and public concern. It is to be hoped that the destruction of the environment by technological interference will be stopped, perhaps reversed, and that this effort has not come too late.

One remembers, according to the ancient legend, that there was something left in Pandora's box, at first overlooked but then visible at the bottom when the many evils that the box had contained had burst forth and flown throughout the world. The name of the entity that still remained was Hope.

7

Planet or
Time Bomb

Even if humanity ceases its unplanned poisoning of the earth, its seas, and its atmosphere, there is a more immediate possibility for ending the world through a spectacular series of explosions, not only ending our present civilization but postponing the development of a new one for thousands of years or perhaps permanently. One hundred and eighteen years ago the young Henry Adams, then assigned to the United States Legation in London, expressed in a letter to his brother in America a view of the future inspired by the state of inventive science in 1862. His outlook was thoroughly enthusiastic, though somewhat contradictory considering the last sentence in the following excerpt:

> I tell you these are great times. Man has mounted science, and is now run away with. I firmly believe that before many centuries more, science will be the master of man. The engines he will have invented will be beyond his strength to control. Some day science may have the existence of mankind in its power, and the human race commit suicide by blowing up the world . . .

Adams was more correct than he probably suspected for, within the last few years only, and for the first time in recorded history, man can literally end the world by pushing a button, an unforeseen and remarkable development of the flowering of our technological civilization.

The scientists who worked on the Manhattan Project foresaw what they were unleashing on the world and sensed that the world would never be the same again. But they were confronted with a "command decision" since they were in a race with the scientists of Nazi Germany who were working on the same sort of project, perhaps for all anyone knew, with a certain lead and, if they were successful first the doubts of the American-based scientists would become moot.

In the face of the reticence of some of the project's scientists, President Roosevelt himself cogently pointed out that failure to develop the bomb would result in the death of the Free World ("The Free World will cease to exist"), an eventuality still to be considered today through the present stockpiling of nuclear weapons.

As described by Walter Sullivan *(Black Holes: 1979)* there were immediate reasons as well as humanitarian ones for the understandable lack of enthusiasm on the part of some of the scientists to explode the first atomic bomb. While Dr. Arthur Compton, from the Chicago Laboratory, suggested that it might even be "better to accept the slavery of the Nazis rather than to run the chance of drawing the final curtain on mankind," the immediate pointed question was whether the explosion might start a self-sustaining chain reaction. If so, it would result in burning off all the earth's atmosphere by causing the nitrogen atom nuclei to fuse into silicon and combine with the oxygen in the air. The atmosphere would then turn into a form of sand and fall back onto the earth. Enrico Fermi, one of the key scientists who participated in the Alamogordo experiment initiated something of a morale problem before the first blast by trying to make a bet with some of the other scientists giving odds on whether or not, when the switch was thrown, the sky would ignite and fall to earth. Dr. Robert Oppenheimer who, through his studies had a wide acquaintance with Sanskrit literature and Hindu legend, suddenly remembered, when the first blast split the sky of New Mexico, a verse from the ancient *Mahabharata* composed thousands of years ago in India but strangely applicable to the nuclear age:

> If the radiance of a thousand suns
> Were to burst at once in the sky,
> That would be like the splendor of the Mighty One . . .
> I am become Death—the destroyer of worlds.

Albert Einstein said it less poetically but more directly when he observed:

> Man now has the power of destruction from which he has no means to protect himself.

Although it has been frequently suggested that nuclear warheads may never again be used in combat since the other side would have them too, history has shown that armies in training and new weapons have always been used. It is a military axiom that for any new weapon there is a counter-weapon or a protective shield. This has been true throughout the ages—for steel swords there were new types of armor; for siege mining there was counter-mining; for tanks, tank traps and armor piercing shells; for gas, gas masks; for aircraft, antiaircraft weapons and radar. Some of the means of warfare that have been "outlawed" such as poison gas and biological (germ) warfare have, it is true, not recently been used by the great powers against each other, not because of their lack of ruthlessness perhaps, but because such substances are so hard to control. Nuclear warfare, however, is an insoluble problem at present, able as it is to kill practically all the troops on both sides and the civilian population as well and to contaminate the field of action as well as neighboring "neutral" countries for an undetermined number of years. It becomes increasingly evident that the only way a superpower can win a conflict is by a first strike, and that even the threat of such a strike would effectively be a cosmic game of Russian roulette. There are enough H-bombs presently stockpiled by the nuclear powers to destroy three million cities the size of (an appropriate example) Hiroshima. Dr. Edward Teller, frequently called "the father of the H-bomb," just as Dr. Oppenheimer was called "the father of the A-bomb," estimates a death toll of about ten million people per H-bomb in metropolitan areas, adding that "a bad nuclear war could kill a couple of billion."

Whether bombs are planned to be delivered by ICBMs, trident submarines, B-52 bombers, cruise missiles, or by satellite, the megaton explosive content increases with the range—the greater the distance the stronger the kill potential. A recent informal conversation the author had with a U.S. general gives an indication of probable military doctrine on either side of the Iron Curtain. From the standpoint of nuclear artillery the general observed:

> If you are going to fire at a 1000-mile plus target you must have knock-out power to a 50- or 100-mile radius. You cannot have an exact landing-on-a-dime target. If we dropped Davey Crockett missiles on a division the effectiveness would depend on whether or not the division was deployed or concentrated. If it were strung out maybe 40 percent would still be around.

> *Question:* Would smaller tactical bombs be the first ones used?

> Military strategy demands that the target be selected to destroy the enemy or incapacitate him to a point where

he will surrender. Someone has to come in first with everything he possesses so that the other nation cannot respond. You pinpoint all the targets and fire all at once to destroy everything.

Question: Why is the neutron bomb considered so ruthless?

It isn't. It has been attacked as a bomb that kills people and spares buildings. But basically it is an offensive weapon that does not contaminate. It kills the enemy by releasing gamma rays without damaging the environment.

Question: Is is true that the hydrogen bomb, if it missed its target and exploded in deep water, might combine with the hydrogen in the water and turn the earth into a sun?

I doubt it. They have been talking about this for years. One man cannot destroy the planet—the forces of nature come into play. Naturally no one is sure.

Among the ever present dangers of nuclear attack is the possibility that a false alarm could be given for a variety of reasons that would trigger an automatic and irrevocable counter-attack. This could arise from a number of causes: an accidental explosion within a country which might appear to be the work of an adversary nation; penetration of air space by unidentified flying objects; accidents in space; or even alerts set off by mistake.

A nuclear explosion in the U.S.S.R. in 1961 caused the destruction of a town in the Urals with considerable contamination in the surrounding area. Fortunately the Soviet authorities realized that the cause was not due to enemy action and directed their efforts to covering up the incident. As for the frequent appearance of UFOs on radar screens and visual sightings, they almost always move too rapidly and erratically to be considered anything more than a temporary aberration. Sustained flights of other kinds have been blamed, on one recent occasion, for having caused a nationwide atomic alert on November 9, 1979. Both U.S. and Canadian jet interceptors took off from their bases under standing orders to attack and destroy during the alert period, which lasted six minutes. Neither the President nor the Joint Chiefs of Staff were alerted during the six minutes. The later official explanation for the alert was that a test tape containing a warning of a simulated Soviet missile attack, which was being played by NORAD for training purposes, was accepted as authentic by interceptors. In a real alert the President would have from twenty to twenty-four minutes (and even less time as delivery systems improve) to determine a course of action before the missiles arrived on their targets.

Besides the official explanation there have been consistent reports that the sudden and dangerous incident was caused by a flight of flocking birds, picked up by radar on the east coast of the United States and communicated to Strategic Air Command Headquarters in Colorado. Although most flights of birds are not dense enough to be confused with ICBMs or aircraft on the National Air Defense Communications Systems, certain flocks of blackbirds, cowbirds, or starlings, massed together in one or several huge flights, and each following a rough V-pattern, might suggest on radar that something of considerable size was approaching.

Comment among Air Force pilots places the area of the first radar warning over Chesapeake Bay. This would be a logical place for migratory flights of birds and also for missiles, from a target point of view, since Washington is not far away.

Another reputed contributing cause for the error was the report that the radar was being adjusted at the time the migratory birds almost started a nuclear countdown. One Navy pilot had expressed his opinion of why the Air Force is unwilling to ascribe the incident to flights of birds:

> They don't like to say it's birds because it makes us look like fools. If birds can fake us, anything else can.

This observation does not suggest inefficiency, as it can be applied to any defense perimeter of any nation. One contemplates with dismay how many more possibilities of annihilation by error will exist as more and more nations join the no longer exclusive atomic club.

Robert Cryer, a British legislator, made his own comment on the November 9 incident:

> The false alert shows beyond doubt that some [nuclear weapons] will sooner or later be used and then there will be no winners because we shall all be losers as part of a radioactive cinder heap.

Further progress on the way to the "cinder heap" was noted on June 3 and again on June 6, 1980 when a slight mistake in the computer warning system indicated that Soviet ballistic missiles had been launched against the United States causing an almost immediate worldwide alert of U.S. strategic nuclear forces. The June 3 alert lasted for three minutes and was cancelled in the fourth leaving relatively few minutes to go before U.S. retaliation and, of course, counter-retaliation. It later appeared that the false alert stemmed from the failure of an electronic component costing about forty-six cents. Assistant Secretary of Defense Gerald P. Dinneen as quoted by the New York *Times* later observed, " . . . we have decided to improve the error detection and correction capabilities of the NORAD communications system."

Another Doomsday effect of nuclear warfare stems from the apparent inability of any power to protect the technique of making thermonuclear bombs. It has frequently been observed in Intelligence circles that any secret weapon developed in the U.S. or the U.S.S.R. would soon become common knowledge: in the case of the United States someone would publish an exposé which would result in a Congressional Investigation, while in the U.S.S.R. it would be released by the government itself for reasons of Russian pride of discovery.

On the American scene a case in point is the recent brouhaha over articles which appeared in a college newspaper and in a local Wisconsin magazine and subsequently in several other papers which might be classified as a do-it-yourself course on how to construct a hydrogen bomb. (The possible employment of such home-made bombs by terrorist groups, small nations, or minorities within larger nations is thought-provoking.) The publications in question, the Wisconsin magazine *The Progressive* and the *Daily Californian,* a campus paper of the University of California, contained, according to a United States Government action brought against the publications, information which was in violation of the Atomic Energy Act of 1954. Such information was based on letters written by Charles Hansen, a California computer programmer with two years of college engineering, who claimed he had used as his sources unrestricted information including encyclopedias, textbooks dealing with the development of nuclear weapons, affidavits released by the government, and his own powers of reasoning. In September 1979 the government action against *The Progressive* was abandoned after a decision by Assistant Attorney-General John H. Shenefield that the secrets underlying the dispute had already been made public.

Terrence B. Adamson, a spokesman for the Department of Justice, protested that publication of the information in the articles "significantly increases the possible spreading of nuclear weapons."

Although the legal decision was generally praised by

newspapers in the United States as favoring "freedom of the press" the incident poses an interesting problem—namely the question of whether the press should publicize information which might be dangerous to the national welfare which, of course, includes the welfare of the national press as well.

With the constant proliferation of nuclear development throughout the planet, however, it is evident that little about nuclear energy, productive or offensive, can long remain a secret. George Rathgens, a political science professor at MIT has pointed out: "By the end of the century" (again 2000 A.D.!) "there will be several thousand nuclear reactors around the world, each producing enough material to build a weapon a week." And with the amount of personnel already operating at so many nuclear plants in the U.S. and elsewhere, not only the knowledge but also the raw material is more or less conveniently at hand for potential private collectors. (According to government reports, enough plutonium has been lost or stolen from a single plant at Savannah River, South Carolina, to build eighteen nuclear bombs.)

There are enough nuclear bombs on hand to make the prophecy of Doomsday a reality in the near future. In the case of the two major contestants only it has been pointed out by Fred Warshofsky that "the United States possesses nuclear capacity to destroy every U.S.S.R. city of 100,000 population 36 times," adding that the Russians could destroy "all the U.S. cities of over 100,000 population only 12 times" (a seeming Russian disadvantage of doubtful consolation to the inhabitants of American cities.)

Worldwide realization of what might happen any day, hour, or minute has certainly contributed to the general psychological malaise experienced by people, especially the young, throughout the world. It even affects Dr. Teller who, although he has consistently favored the hydrogen bomb as a means of protecting the U.S. and the Free World, is understandably preoccupied about its being used. He has said: "Although I have never dreamed—recently I have dreamt of the war that will come." Many of us may come to share Dr. Teller's dreams.

As more and more nations develop nuclear weapons it seems logical to assume that they will eventually use them. At the present moment the U.S., the U.S.S.R., Great Britain, France, and China possess thermonuclear weapons (with India having an A-bomb) and all these countries proclaim the importance of their manufacture and testing as a necessary "deterrent." Other nations are even now studying their development and most probably working on them. These include Israel and South Africa, both suspected of an atomic test in the South Atlantic; Pakistan, resentful of India's atomic prestige, which feels the world needs an exclusively Islamic bomb, and the Federal Republic of Germany, thought to be making atomic tests in Africa. Japan, one of the world's greatest industrial powers, may soon desire to develop its own atomic defense, despite or because of its unhappy memories. Other countries on a possible atomic list because of their industrial potential, desire for prestige, protection, or fulfillment of national aims include Libya, Venezuela, Saudi Arabia, Brazil, Mexico, Argentina, Algeria, Indonesia, Australia, and New Zealand. National or international groups will soon be able to procure nuclear bombs from possessor nations sympathetic to their aims, or even construct them in secret, A secret CIA report quoted by columnist Jack Anderson allegedly states:

> None of the individual steps involved would be beyond the capabilities of a sophisticated, well-funded group.

It has been calculated by nuclear experts that in the near future at least thirty-four nations will be members of the nuclear club, with all the attendant possibilities of devastating or even blowing up the planet. The estimated date?—2000 A.D.

It took our present civilization approximately 6,000 years to pregress from primitive agriculture to the development of the atom bomb—from comparative barbarism to the beginning of the control or unleashing of the forces of the universe. Mankind, however, whose age is now reckoned not in thousands but in millions of years, has had a developed brain potential, at least for the last 100,000 years, which is the equal to that of modern man (some Cro-Magnon skulls even show a brain capacity superior to that of modern man). I believe scientists accept as fact that the cubic capacity of the skull has no direct relation to potential or actual intelligence. Within the last twenty years of archaelogical land and underwater exploration, it has become increasingly obvious that there have been previous civilizations so old that we do not know their names, stretching well back into the nighttime of history before our own historic dawn of approximately 4000 B.C. If these prior civilizations developed a system of scientific progress—not necessarily the same but comparable to ours—they would have had ample time to develop a technological society which could have led them to explore and use the power of the atom and be faced, as we are now, with the same choice of control or destruction. Perhaps this is a normal progression of a constantly advancing civilization—to advance until it destroys itself.

Certain cultural records preserved in early historic and religious literature, partially corroborated by some curious archaelogical discoveries, appear to indicate that something resembling atomic bombs were employed in warfare on this planet thousands of years before present recorded history began. We did not recognize these detailed references to nuclear warfare in ancient legends until we ourselves developed atomic power.

Most of these references come from the *Mahabharata,* the *Ramayana,* the Puranic and Vedic texts, the *Mahavira Charita* and other Sanskrit texts which, unlike the burnings and destructions suffered by most books of Mediterranean and Middle Eastern antiquity, have come down to us directly from ancient times. The "atomic" references they contained were generally considered by Westerners, since the first complete translation of the *Mahabharata* in 1843 (it was originally written in Sanskrit in 1500 B.C. from legends dating 5,000 years before that), to be simply examples of fervid oriental imaginings of wars of gods and ancient heroes.

It was only after the atomic explosions in 1945 and subsequently that a gradual realization or recognition of what they really described began to take place among those familiar with these ancient works. They seemed to be referring to specific details of atomic warfare and its effects and represented either an unbelievable memory of the past or an eerie prophecy of the future.

Only seven years after the first successful atom bomb blast in New Mexico, Dr. Oppenheimer, who was familiar with ancient Sanskrit literature, was giving a lecture at Rochester University. During the question and answer period a student asked a question to which Oppenheimer gave a strangely qualified answer.

Student: Was the bomb exploded at Alamogordo during the Manhattan Project the first one to be detonated?

Dr. Oppenheimer: Well—yes. In modern times, of course.

Perhaps Dr. Oppenheimer was remembering a passage he had read in the *Mahabharata* about an ancient

war in which a new and terrifying weapon was introduced:

> (It was) a single projectile
> Charged with all the power of the Universe.
> An incandescent column of smoke and flame
> As bright as ten thousand Suns
> Rose in all its splendor . . .
> . . . It was an unknown weapon,
> An iron thunderbolt,
> A gigantic messenger of death,
> Which reduced to ashes
> The entire race of the Vrishnis and the Andhakas.
> . . . The corpses were so burned
> As to be unrecognizable.
> Their hair and nails fell out;
> Pottery broke without apparent cause,
> And the birds turned white.
> After a few hours
> All foodstuffs were infected . . .
> . . . To escape from this fire
> The soldiers threw themselves in streams
> To wash themselves and their equipment . . .

The dimensions of this legendary weapon bear a certain resemblance to present-day tactical atomic missiles.

> . . . A shaft fatal as the rod of death.
> It measured three cubes and six feet.
> Endowed with the force
> Of thousand-eyed Indra's thunder,
> It was destructive of all living creatures . . .

The powerful effects of the blast and the heat generated by this weapon are described in an imaginative
and lyrical manner but one which could apply (except
for the elephants) to the dropping of an atomic bomb.

. . . Then (the god of that mighty weapon)
Bore away crowds of Samsaptakas
With steeds and elephants and cars and weapons,
As if these were dry leaves of trees . . .
Borne away by the wind, O King,
They looked highly beautiful
Like flying birds flying away from trees . . .

And further,

. . . Inauspicious winds began to blow . . .
The Sun seemed to turn around,
The Universe, scorched with heat,
Seemed to be in a fever.
Elephants and other creatures of the land,
Scorched by the energy of that weapon,
Ran in flight . . .
The very waters being heated,
The creatures living in that element
Began to burn . . .
Hostile warriors fell down like trees
Burnt down in a raging fire . . .
Huge elephants burnt by that weapon,
Fell down on the earth . . .
. . . Uttering fierce cries . . .
Others scorched by the fire ran hither and yon,
As in the midst of a forest conflagration,
The steeds . . . and the chariots also,
Burnt by the energy of that weapon . . .
Looked like the tops of trees
Burnt in a forest fire . . .

As if the minute descriptions of something very
much resembling atomic bombing were not coincidental enough, there has come down to us from the
ancient *Mahabharata* a sort of antibomb protest:

. . . A substance like fire
Has sprung into existence

Even now blistering hills and rivers and trees.
. . . All kinds of herbs and grass
 In the mobile and immobile Universe
Are being reduced to ashes . . .

. . . You cruel and wicked ones,
Intoxicated with pride,
Through that iron bolt you will become
(The) exterminators of your race . . .

One is reminded of the yet unknown final effect of a super-bomb when we read in the *Ramayana* of a projectile:

. . . So powerful that it could destroy
The earth in an instant—
A great soaring sound in smoke and flames . . .
And on it sits Death . . .

One wonders whether these imaginative but somehow plausible references, transmitted to the present time by the classics of India, are based on a memory of their use by some prior civilization—a people that used this power and through its use brought about its own destruction. Subsequently a passage in the *Samarangana Sutradhara of Bhoja* deals with the *decline* of artillery weapons of thousands of years *before* the time of writing, implying a return to simpler forms of warfare in semihistoric times. We do not know, of course, whether a prehistoric culture may or may not have employed proto-atomic bombs although there exist some rather disquieting indications outside the field of religious poetry.

In Pakistan, in what used to be the Indus Valley of India, there are ruins of several ancient cities that are credited with having contained, within their immense areas, populations of well over a million each. They are not mentioned in history: we can assume that they existed before our recorded history. The largest are now called Mohenjo-Daro and Harappa, although we have no idea what their names were when they flourished. Their system of writing has never been deciphered, although it has been found in another area—at Easter Island in the Pacific, exactly on the other side of the world. Apparently both of these cities were destroyed suddenly; excavations down to the street level have revealed scattered skeletons, as if doom had come so swiftly that the inhabitants did not have time to get to their houses. These skeletons, after unknown thousands of years, are still among the most radioactive that have ever been found, on a par with those of Hiroshima and Nagasaki.

One might observe, in view of her long familiarity

A possible end of civilization as might be seen from space without cloud cover. Although it has been suggested that a concentrated nuclear attack on a single section of the earth might conceivably throw the planet off its axis, an almost immediate counterattack would scatter the jolting explosions—perhaps to the advantage of the earth although not to its inhabitants.

with the "legends" of the Iron Thunderbolt, that India might have been expected to show more reticence before she joined the atomic powers through the underground explosion of her first atomic bomb (or perhaps the first after 8,000 years?) in Rajasthan, in May of 1974.

8

Has the World Ended Before?

If atomic warfare were actually used in the distant past and not just imagined, there must still exist some indications of a civilization advanced enough to develop or even to know about atomic power. One does find in some of the ancient writings of India some descriptions of advanced scientific thinking which seemed anachronistic to the age from which they come. The *Jyotish* (4000 B.C.) echoes the modern concept of the earth's place in the universe, the law of gravity, the kinetic nature of energy, and the theory of cosmic rays and also deals, in specialized but unmistakable vocabulary, with the theory of atomic rays. And that was thousands of years before the medieval theologians of Europe argued about the number of angels that could fit on the head of a pin. Indian philosophers of the *Vaisesika** school were discussing atomic theory, speculating about heat being the cause of molecular change, and calculating the period of time taken by an atom to traverse its own space. Readers of the Buddhist Pali sutras and commentaries, who studied them before modern times, were frequently mystified by reference to the "tying together" of minute component parts of matter; although nowadays it is

---

* Translation: *Vaisesika*—"atomatic individuality"

135

easy for a modern reader to recognize an understandable description of molecular composition.

This awareness of the composition of matter and with it an advanced concept of mathematics extended to different parts of the earliest ancient world, although it seemed considerably to diminish and finally to be lost as time progressed. It can be noted in the remarkable measurements of the Great Pyramid of Egypt, the mathematical calculations of the Sumerians and Babylonians who easily dealt with figures in the quadrillions, although later developing races forgot or never knew the use of zero and counted only in thousands or even multiples of twenty (twenty being the total count of fingers plus toes). We see this in the astronomical knowledge of the ancient Maya who, like the Sumerians, were somehow familiar with stars and planets which cannot be seen without telescopes, and who knew the use of zero and calculated with surprising exactness the true duration of the solar year thousands of years before modern man attained the presently accepted figure (Maya count: 365.2420 days; modern count: 365.2422 days).

The scientific knowledge of matter and the cosmos extant in some parts of the ancient world seems to have been present on a high level almost at the beginning and then to have slid into a decline as if something had happened to cause civilization and knowledge to run backward. It was as if a great catastrophe occurred and that isolated groups on the world's surface had retained bits of an advanced culture and had then gradually lost them after being cut off from the source.

While Greece and Rome were developing new civilizations the vestiges of an older one, seemingly worldwide in scope, was vanishing. It left incomprehensible texts, which only today are understandable in terms of modern technology, and curious artifacts so modern in concept that we cannot believe that the ancients invented them. Since there is no place for them in what we consider the stream of history we prefer either to ignore their function, consider them imports from other worlds in space, or to catalog them as ornaments or "ritual objects."

An attractive theory exists, supported by Erich von Däniken *(Chariots of the Gods?)* and other writers, that the anachronistic and surprising evidence of advanced civilization in the ancient world can be explained by the influence and help of visits by extraterrestrials. These humanoid explorers, operating as a sort of cosmic Peace Corps, brought civilized ways to the undeveloped people of the planet Earth, evidently considered by the visitors as a planet in need of extraterrestrial aid. While not denying that the earth may have been visited by space beings either in the remote past or even in the present, there is still no definite way to establish the truth of this comfortable theory, which implies that we were watched over in the past and will probably be watched over in the future. It seems more logical however, that with at least 100,000 or more years of mankind having the mental capacity to develop a world civilization, Earth people might well have done so more than once and, when and if it suffered destruction, for some to survive and start the whole process anew.

This concept was well known to some of the races of antiquity and was well expressed by Plato 2,000 years ago when he quoted an Egyptian priest in a conversation with the Athenian law giver, Solon, who is supposed to have said about the Greeks:

> . . . in mind you are all young; there is no old opinion handed down among you by ancient tradition, nor any science that is hoary with age. And I will tell you the reason . . . there have been and will be again many destructions of mankind arising out of many causes . . .

later adding

At the usual period the stream from the heavens descends like a pestilence and leaves only those of you who are destitute of letters and education; and thus you have to begin all over again as children; and know nothing of what happened in ancient times either among us or among yourselves . . .

In the first place you remember one deluge only, whereas there were many of them . . .

Besides allusions to the Deluge in the Bible and the books and traditions of many nations, there are concrete references that have subsisted for thousands of years, indicating an acceptance of pre-flood civilization by ancient cultures. King Ashurbanipal of Assyria was referring to relics from a civilization that to him was already "prehistoric" when he had written for posterity:—"I understand the enigmatic words in the stone carvings from the days before the Deluge."

Even the unexplainable artifacts from former ages seem to parallel our own discoveries with the exception that they come from several thousand years ago. Among the more sensational are gold models of what strongly resemble delta-winged planes found in Colombian tombs from 1,500 years ago: even older glider models from ancient Egypt were finally recognized as such although long thought to be toy birds; dry cell batteries from Babylon and Nineveh which still work after 2,500 years when the electrolyte is added; a wall panel in Dendera, Egypt, showing recognizable giant light bulbs attached with braided cables to a generator which would incidentally, explain the lighting system of the interiors of the deep Egyptian tombs; even a bronze object found at the bottom of the Aegean Sea which, years later, was found to be a star computer, changing the whole concept of ancient navigation.

A geared and wheeled model very similar in form to an excavator, made of gold, was found in Panama; magnifying lenses from ruins in ancient Assyria and also from pre-Columbian Ecuador; and the imprints of a number of iron nails or screws found in deep layers within the earth in South America, from a geological era thousands of years before iron was thought to have been employed. These are only a few of a constantly growing list of new finds and newly recognized artifacts that had been long available in museums and collections. People, of course, could not recognize planes, computers, earth movers, electricity, or atom bombs before they were officially invented.

A further ghostly reminder of the vanished civilizations of prehistory are vast building complexes constructed of stones so huge that we cannot understand how they were moved to the building site and set together with such precision without the use of modern building equipment. They are standing enigmas: the Great Pyramid of Egypt; a stone foundation which was used by the Romans as a base for the Temple of Jupiter at Baalbek in Lebanon, although the Romans never found out what was originally on the foundation where stones weighing up to four million pounds each were exactly fitted together. Other standing stone giants include the great Sarsen stones at Stonehenge and the thirty-mile stone zodiac calendar in Glastonbury, England; the huge menhirs of Carnac, France, some of which continue out in lines underneath the sea; the prehistoric stone forts of Western Ireland and the Isle of Aran, where some of the stones are fused together as if once hit by the equivalent of a present-day atomic blast; the cyclopean ruins of prehistoric Spain and pre-Hellenic Greece.

The enormous but perfectly fitted boulders of Sacsahuaman, Peru, were built so long before the time of the Incas that the Incas attributed them to the gods. When an earthquake on May 21, 1950, at Cuzco, Peru, split one of these incredible walls, it was revealed that the inside of the split was curved, smooth, and exactly fitted from outside to inside the enormously thick walls, implying a technological perfection seldom achieved in buildings today, even with the use of the most sophisticated modern equipment.

In Bolivia there still stands the stone city of Tiahuanaco, so old that its broken pottery shows pictures of Pleistocene animals. Although Tiahuanaco is now at an altitude of 13,500 feet, too high for a population to live, its docks and quays indicate that it was once a seaport and that it rose *with the Andes* when they were created 11,000 years ago. All of these cyclopean ruins have a striking similarity, as if the same builders had positioned and shaped these great boulders in accord with now forgotten laws of alignment.

In Peru, mountain peaks at Marcahuasi have been carved into the shapes of great animals, some of them by now extinct in South America, by sculptors who apparently handled stone as if they were modeling in clay. A giant stone jaguar in the Loltún Caves of Yucatan, completely different in concept from later Amerindian art forms, has revealed petrified sea fauna in its pitted carvings, demonstrating that it had been long immersed below sea level and had surfaced again as it followed the heavings of the land into and out of the sea.

It is perhaps in the sea itself that proof will be found of the world civilization that may have existed before this present one. Since the development of underwater exploration, air-sea operations, and submarine photography, a number of remains of prehistoric buildings have been found under the sea, generally by chance, and often in unexpected places. Or perhaps they were not completely unexpected since the imagination of man has been concerned with the legend of the sinking of Atlantis for more than 2,000 years, one of humanity's oldest and most persistent traditions closely connected as it is with the memory of a world catastrophe—the Great Flood.

An increasing number of prehistoric archaeological

sites have been found in the Atlantic Ocean, almost exactly where Plato said the lost empire of Atlantis had flourished before its sudden destruction 11,000 years ago. In Plato's words:

> . . . in those days the Atlantic was navigable; and there was an island situated in front of the straits which you call the Columns of Herakles (Gibraltar and Mt. Atlas) . . . the island was larger than Libya and Asia put together, and was the way to other islands, and from the islands you might pass through the whole of the opposite continent which surrounded the true ocean; for this sea which is within the Straits of Herakles (the Mediterranean) is only a harbor, having a narrow entrance, but that other is a real sea, and the surrounding land may be most truly called a continent. Now, in the island of Atlantis there was a great and wonderful empire . . .

It may be logically and intellectually satisfying, of course, to accept Plato's account as a pleasant fable, as many scholars have done throughout the centuries and as the scientific establishment of today still does. But it would be more difficult to do so if remains of cities were found under the Atlantic Ocean, whose very name recalls Atlantis.

In any case it is interesting to note that whether Plato was correct or not in his reports about Atlantis he was undeniably right about the continent on the other side of "the real sea"—the Atlantic Ocean. Plato's dialogues concerning Atlantis were familiar to and served as an inspiration to Columbus, who was advised in a letter from one of his correspondents as he was preparing for his epic voyage, that he would probably find some vestiges of Atlantis still above sea level when he reached the middle of the ocean, and that on those surviving islands he might be able to repair and resupply his ships.

If the present Atlantic islands are really, as legends claim, the tops of the former mountains of Atlantis still protruding from the sea, then the sea bottom near these islands might be expected to reveal vestiges of an ancient ruined civilization, so old, according to our own 6,000-year time frame of accepted history, as to be "historically impossible" as well as disturbing to the academic establishment. But this is what is now happening on different parts of the floor of the Atlantic.

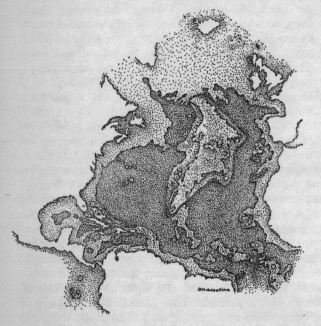

View of the possible land mass of Atlantis based on present oceanic depths. The 1,000-foot level of the Atlantic is indicated by the light dotted concentrations, which would give a fairly accurate picture of the Atlantic Ocean at about 11,000 B.C. before the melting of the glaciers raised the sea level. The Atlantic would have then been easier to traverse, with numerous island stopping places from east to west until, as Plato related in his dialogues, the "opposite continent" on the other side of "the true ocean" could be reached.

The presence of underwater ruins in the open ocean, as opposed to exploration of sunken cities or parts of cities in the Mediterranean, which have sunk or collapsed into the sea in historic times, is contrary to the history of civilization as we know it. But it is not contrary to the history of the planet earth. Something of considerable force happened about 11,000 years ago, causing the glaciers to melt, killing off millions of animals throughout the world and leaving an unforgettable memory among human survivors of the apparent end of the world through flood and fire. Ruins on the ocean floor, especially in the Atlantic, would seem to establish that such structures would have existed before the last time the ocean rose, as a result of the last sudden glaciation.

The sites at which a series of stone buildings, stairways, fortifications, walls, docks, and roads have been found under the Atlantic might be said to form a rough outline of the reputed "Atlantean" empire, even to the stepping stones of lesser islands, as mentioned by Plato, leading to the "opposite continent." Starting in a great arc from the north coast of South America we find mention of a one-hundred-mile long "wall" in the ocean off Venezuela, refused credence as an artifact because it is "too long" to be other than a natural formation. Off the coast of Belize and Yucatan, causeways that have vanished on land can be seen still to run beneath the sea until they vanish into the deep water. In the sea north of Cuba there is a ruin which spreads over several acres and seems to be of marble. About forty miles south of Florida there is a huge object which has the shape of a four-sided pyramid, at a depth from the surface of several hundred feet, that has been outlined by sonar and indistinctly though convincingly by closed circuit television. On the banks of the Bahamas there are, in the opinion of Dr. Manson Valentine who discovered (1968) the now well-known "Bimini wall" or road, there are scores of sites of ancient constructions lying underwater which were built by no race known to history. The Bimini road or wall appears to be an underwater causeway whose giant blocks of stone resemble the megalithic constructions of South America and Europe. This 3,000-foot-long artifact gives an indication of being much longer, as the same line of stone vanishes under the sea bottom and then reappears at other places around the island of Bimini as if it once surrounded the whole island forming a citadel or acropolis.

Concept by Dr. Valentine of the undersea formation, similar to a pyramid (based on sonar readings and closed circuit TV), located 300 feet below the surface, 40 miles at sea, off the southern coast of Florida. The top of this assumed artifact does not end in a point like the Great Pyramid of Gizeh, but may support the ruins of a small temple. Unusual as the presence of an underwater pyramid off the coast of the United States may appear, this is but one of many archaeological sites from the Yucatan to the Bahamas which evince the onetime presence of an extensive culture which sank under or was covered by the sea as a result of a cataclysm. Some of these artifacts are close enough to the ocean's surface to be the subject of current exploration.

In deeper water, further out into the ocean, a complex system of standing walls, one of which has a curved archway opening, exists on the ocean floor along with raised stone platforms and step pyramids reported to be of considerable size. West of Andros three great concentric circles formed by a series of standing stones has been photographed from the air and a smaller version of triple walls has recently been found in fairly shallow water on the Bahama Banks. Due south of Andros straight lines visible from the air run underwater as if they traced ancient roads running along the former coastline on a cliff which is now under the ocean. On the precipitous continental shelf off Andros officers of a French submersible, the *Archimède*, observed in 1964 what appeared to be a wide stone stairway cut in the continental shelf itself at a depth of over 1,000 feet, as if the stairway once ascended from the sea coast to a high plateau—now the low-lying island of Andros.

Off the coast of the eastern United States an apparent roadway of undetermined length exists on the ocean floor off Georgia; a ten-mile wall has been charted off the coast of Delaware; and standing stone walls and a round tower have been discovered by divers off Rhode Island at an ocean depth of forty to fifty feet.

In the central Atlantic Ocean, south of the Azores, where the main island of Atlantis is customarily located by legend, World War II air ferry pilots engaged in transporting planes to the war zones, reported seeing, when the sun's rays were slanted for maximum visibility and the water was clear, what seemed to be underwater cities at an estimated depth of eighty to one hundred twenty feet below the surface. In this area underwater sea mounts and plateaus rise from great depths almost to the surface while former sand beaches exist a mile below.

Extending the arc toward Europe, we find accounts of underwater ruins and inscriptions in the sea around the Canary Islands (whose original inhabitants thought they were the only survivors of a global catastrophe); and cyclopean walls extending for miles underwater off the coast of Morocco into the Atlantic.

Recently published claims (and, more importantly, photographs) have been the result of a Soviet expedition engaged in making studies of the sea floor in the Atlantic Ocean near Madeira. The photographs were taken from the SS *Academician Petrovsky* in 1974 on the flat top of the Ampère Seamount at a depth of 600 feet. Although the expedition was not archaeological but oceanographic, Vladimir Marakuev of the U.S.S.R. Institute of Oceanography and responsible for the photographs, pointing out that the prints show walls of masonry blocks and a clearly defined giant staircase, has stated:

Nowhere have I seen anything so close to the traces of . . . the activity of man in places that could once have been dry land . . .

While there are submerged prehistoric ruins in other parts of the world, still standing giant walls and step pyramids one and a half miles deep in the Peru-Nazca trench, unidentified undersea ruins off the islands of the South Pacific, Japan, and Southern India, it is probable that all these architectural vestiges are connected with the last great planetary catastrophe, which has become a part of world folklore through the memory of Atlantis. And it is primarily in the former land areas of the Atlantic, now submerged, where proof of the Atlantean legend is being established.

The number of books about Atlantis in all languages is conservatively estimated as 25,000 and is still growing, as humanity searches for a definitive version of its cultural roots. These studies include a variety of disciplines: linguistics, anthropology, zoology, geology, oceanography, seismology, history, philosophy, and religion, to name a few, and the arguments between partisans about the actuality of Atlantis have, in Europe, sometimes ended in bombings and fatalities.

Two favorite refutations by those skeptical of the verity of Atlantis are the statements that Atlantis existed only in the imagination of Plato or that Plato or Solon had got it mixed with the volcanic explosion of Thera, in the Aegean Sea (1500 B.C.). While Plato may have been the chronicler of Atlantis he was far from being the only one, and simply used for his dialogues an account that many ancient scholars were familiar with, in various parts of the Mediterranean and other areas of the world as well.

Even if no other proof of Atlantis than its name existed, one would almost be convinced that there was some truth behind the legend. The map on page 148 shows where the most ancient races, guided by their oldest traditions, thought that an earthly or heavenly paradise existed on an island in the sea, inhabited by superior beings or by the gods themselves. It is notable that the Euro-Africans placed it to the west, while the Amerindian races believed it to lie in the ocean to the east. Most of them believed that their own races or tribes had originally come from this enchanted paradise before it was destroyed by sinking into the ocean. Almost all of them considered it to be a great sea empire which they called by some variant of the word Atlantis, a name generally containing the sounds A, T (or D), L and N. The fact that these names differ, although being linguistically close to each other, show linguistic and regional differences which make the common reference even more convincing.

These three great arcs or circles around the Atlantic, the cyclopean stone ruins on land (only stone could have lasted through so many centuries), the presence of architectural remains under the ocean and on the continental shelves, around the Atlantic islands, and in the oceanic abyss itself, and finally, the similar names given to the sunken continent by the ancient nations surrounding the ocean and the traditions they sub-

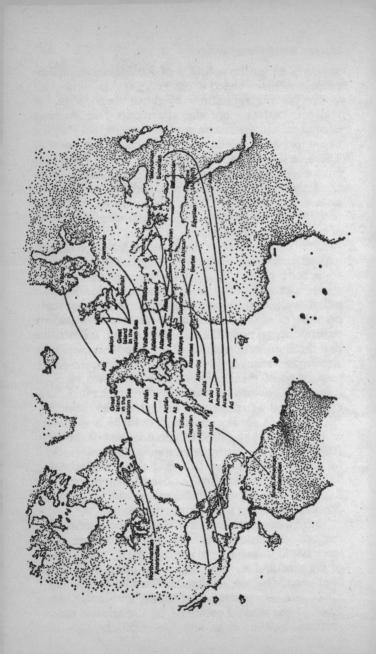

We may never know what Atlantis was really called, although legends and memories from races on both sides of the Atlantic and the Mediterranean ascribe names to a lost land or people that have a convincing similarity even in their disparity. It is interesting to note that the initial sound of the word Atlantis, atl, common to so many traditions, also means water in the language of ancient Mexico and among the Berbers of North Africa. Even the word we use for this part of the world ocean may be said to constitute a further reminder of a dimly remembered but persistent past.

scribed to it, constitute actualities that have stood through the ages to mystify, intrigue, or inspire us.

Meanwhile, archaeologists, oceanographers, and other scientists continue to question the "possibility" of Atlantis having existed at all, either in the Atlantic Ocean or, in "miniature" form in a variety of at least seventy other areas covering all continents and many of the large and small islands in the five oceans. About fifty years ago, Major K. Bilau, a German investigator of the Atlantis tradition, contributed an enthusiastic declaration which might be considered a typical conviction on the part of the Atlantic "Atlantologists." He wrote:

Deep under the ocean's waters Atlantis is now reposing and only its highest summits are still visible in . . . the Azores. Its cold and hot springs, described by the ancient authors still flowing there as they flowed many millenia ago. The mountain lakes of Atlantis have been transformed now into submerged ones. If we follow exactly Plato's indications and seek the site of Poseidonis among the half-submerged summits of the Azores, we will find it to the south of the island of Dollabarata. There, upon an eminence in the middle of a large and comparatively straight valley, which was well protected from the winds, stood the capital, center of an unknown prehistoric culture . . . It is strange that the scientists have sought Atlantis everywhere, but have given the least attention to this spot, which after all, was closely indicated by Plato.

Since the time Major Bilau wrote his exuberant opinion, sonar soundings of the ocean have established a much clearer picture of the ocean bottom. The general results of this information would doubtlessly have caused Bilau considerable satisfaction. The map on page 142 shows three plateaus in the Central Atlantic; one at a depth of about 2,000 feet, another at 1,000 feet, and a smaller, shallower plateau surrounding the shores of the Azores islands at the surface. The 1,000 feet plus level could be explained by the increase of water in the ocean since the melting of the last glaciers, and would also indicate that the other Atlantic islands, such as Madeira, the Canaries, the Cape Verde group, the Bahamas, Bermuda and other islands would have had much larger land surfaces. Other islands and sea mounts now beneath the surface would be above sea level, further increasing land area in the Atlantic as Plato reported it in his dialogues.

The deeper 2,000 feet plus level could indicate a catastrophic convulsion which caused the land mass to descend precipitously into the sea, a phenomenon suggested by the sandy beaches (once a shoreline) which have been found off the Azores at a depth of thousands of feet.

But besides information contained in new depth maps there exist other maps, copies and recopies from the dawn of historic times, passing into our hands from ancient Greece and Egypt but evidently compiled at a considerably earlier period, which show coastlines and the interiors of continents whose features the original cartographers, according to what we believe of history, could not possibly have known. These ancient maps show geographical features that have ceased to exist or have been covered over by ice; in other words, the maps show an earlier world the way it once was.

While maps are an indication, although not a proof, of the scientific and geographical knowledge of an "Atlantean world," if they are authentic they constitute a definite proof that some civilization before history understood and used spheroid trigonometry for establishing longitude in map-making (not rediscovered until the reign of George III) and was capable of sailing (or flying?) to the farthest sections of the world, leaving maps that showed that their makers had an excellent idea of the earth's complete topography including some features not rediscovered by modern man until the middle of the twentieth century.

The term "rediscovered" is a pertinent one, for apparently the makers of these maps at a period which we consider the very beginning or before the beginning of history, were already aware of the roundness of the earth and capable of figuring latitude and longitude enabling them to voyage to and explore the most remote parts of the world at a point so far back in time that glaciers still covered the northern lands, the Antarctic was largely ice free, the Sahara was not yet a desert but was fertile, flourishing, and endowed with rivers and lakes, and vestiges of large Atlantic islands were still above the surface of the ocean.

These maps, commonly called portolano charts, were largely kept as secret as possible by ancient and medieval seafarers before the voyages of the Age of Discovery produced new maps, based at first on copies of the old charts. The originals, which were more correct than the copies, had been burned in the destruction of the great libraries of the ancient world in Alexandria, Carthage, and other cities of Greece and the Roman Empire. But some surviving copies were passed down hand to hand through a relatively tight group of captains, navigators, and merchants, jealously guarded for some time and finally redrawn under the name of the most recent copyist or owner. These maps were, of course, infinitely superior to the regular maps made in the Middle Ages, many depicting the earth as flat, and both earth and sea filled with monsters.

Columbus is said to have possessed and used a

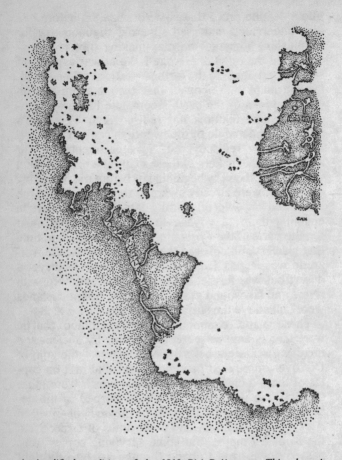

A simplified rendition of the 1513 Piri Re'is map. This chart is reported to have been copied and recopied from maps used more than 2,000 years ago by the ancient Greeks, Phoenicians and Minoans, who apparently had inherited them from unknown predecessors thousands of years before their time. The desert area of Africa, upper right, is shown as a land of rivers and lakes, which it once was, and the coast of Antarctica, lower center and apparently connected to South America, is shown as it was before the ice covered it.

source copy of the famous Piri Re'is map. A surviving copy (1513) is named after a Turkish sea captain who had the information copied. This map, made from an original many centuries before 1513 showed, across the Atlantic Ocean, Cuba and other recognizable islands of the Caribbean, Central America, and the east and west coasts of South America, including the Andes, as well as parts of Antarctica, many centuries before any of these features had been discovered, as far as we know, by explorers from the Old World. Piri Re'is, in describing the map, stated that it was copied from an original from Alexandria (where the conquering Moslems almost a thousand years previously had burned a million and a half book manuscripts to heat the baths of the city).

The finding of the Piri Re'is map and much of the subsequent recognition of the portolano maps came about by chance. The map, inked and painted on antelope skin, was found in the Topkapi Palace at Istanbul after the hasty departure of the last Sultan of Turkey. Eventually a copy came to the attention of a map expert, Captain A. H. Mallery, U.S.N., who noted that the bottom of this antique map correctly showed part of the coastline of Antarctica—but a part *now* under the ice. It revealed mountain ranges and rivers, now under ice risers and glaciers, which we, through the aid of modern devices, know are there, although it is difficult to understand how ancient map makers did unless they mapped Antarctica *before* the ice covered it 8,000 to 10,000 years ago.

Following the Mallery studies of the map, Professor Charles Hapgood devoted the better part of a lifetime in the comparative examination of the Piri Re'is and other portolano maps to establish the correlation of ancient and modern coordinates. He was able to prove that these maritime charts showed scientific knowledge greatly superior to that of the Middle Ages and comparable to that of our relatively modern map ex-

pertise which began only with the successful calculation of longitude in the early nineteenth century.

Copies of some of these other ancient maps have
substantiated the fact that the world was much better
known by ancient and even medieval mariners than we
have heretofore believed. Many of these charts, by a
correct placing of recognizable coastlines and islands,
demonstrate that seamen of ancient times were able to
navigate not only by the stars but by mathematics as
well, and that they had a spherical concept of the earth
which, despite the legends, few navigators believed to
be flat. When sometimes the coastlines and other
features are not in agreement with present data, we
now know that they were correct at the time they were
drawn thousands of years ago. They show information
about certain sections of the earth which the map

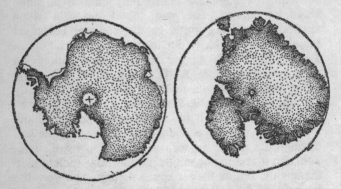

*The Antarctic continent as it is (left) and as represented in the
Oranteus Finaeus map of 1532 (right). The position of the North
Pole on the Finaeus map is represented as northeast of where it
presently is. The location of the pole has changed in the thousands
of years since the ancient maps which Finaeus copied were originally drawn. As in the case of other ancient and medieval maps of
Antarctica, the Europeans who copied them knew of a southern
continent only as a myth and simply reproduced what they found on
ancient Greek or Phoenician maps. An especially interesting feature
of the map is the indicated presence of rivers and fjords, which were
evidently visited by extremely ancient mariners before the continent
was covered by ice 7,000 to 9,000 years ago.*

makers must have personally observed when part of the earth's geological features and climate had not yet changed or were changing, a period so far in the past that it is difficult to believe that intelligent observers, let alone map makers, were present at the time.

In 1532 Orance Finé (Oranteus Finaeus) a cartographer invited to the court of François I of France, copied and designed a world map including a fairly accurate Antarctica with coasts and mountain ranges corresponding to those discovered in recent years although Antarctica was not officially discovered until the nineteenth century. Although he placed the South Pole at some distance from its true location, this would not be inconsistent, considering the time lapse, with the changing positions of the poles.

A map designed by Iehudi Ibn ben Zara in Alexandria in 1487 indicates remnants of glaciers in the British Isles, and detailed profiles of islands in the Mediterranean and Aegean Seas which are still there—but underwater.

The Hamy King chart (1502) shows the rivers of Northern Siberia flowing into the Arctic Ocean, all of which area is now under ice. Great islands in Southeast Asia, now separated are shown as connected by land, as we know they once were. South India is depicted as an island, as it could have been for a period because of catastrophic flooding of the northern plains which still contain, as does the Sahara, considerable fossilized evidence of marine life. The Hamy King map has an interesting annotation picked up from Egyptian history—it indicates the canal connecting the Mediterranean with the Red Sea, the original Suez Canal built by the early Egyptian Pharoahs.

Both the Hamy King chart and the Benincasa map of 1508 show glaciation still present in the Baltic countries, while the Zara map depicts Greenland without an ice cap which, although not the case in 1380, was geologically true thousands of years earlier.

In the Hadji Ahmed world map of 1559, the uncharted *west* coast of North America, presumably copied from very ancient maps, is more correct than the east coast, incorrectly modified as it was by reports of early European explorers. Antarctica appears in its correct place and a land bridge apparently connects Alaska and Russia, and Novaya Zemlaya is

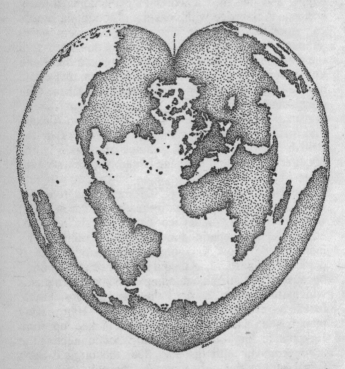

Copy of the Hadji Ahmed globe of 1559, taken from ancient Greek sources, showing an elongated Antarctic continent at the unknown bottom of the world and a surprisingly exact map of the west coast of North America. It is considered that the original of this map, like the Piri Re'is section of a world map, was drawn at a time when the Antarctic was free of ice. Perhaps one of the most striking features of the Hadji Ahmed map is the apparent linking of the Russian coastline to North America.

joined to Siberia—both geological possibilities before the world rising of the waters.

A map by the Greek cartographer, Eratosthenes, while not a portolano chart, was evidently made by him in classical times while the Great Library at Alexandria was still functioning. Eratosthenes' map shows the Caspian Sea opening *north* to the Arctic, now 1,000 miles away—an apparent impossibility, although not completely so, for even today there are Arctic seals in the Caspian.

Philippe Buache was among the map makers of the Age of Discovery who admitted that they copied information from the ancient portolano maps. In 1739 Buache published a map of the southern hemisphere—basing his concept upon a possible southern continent which many thought should be there "to balance the other land masses." The continent he came up with corresponds remarkably to a correct concept of Antarctica except that the land was divided into two great islands. This detail seemed to be simply an imaginative touch until it was found, in a multinational geodectic survey of 1958, to be nothing less than fact; if the ice were not there the continent would be split by a seaway running between the Ross and Weddell Seas. For past explorers to have known this they would have had to visit Antartica at least 8,000 years earlier before the climate changed and the ice covered the shoreline.

Many of the portolano charts showed unidentified and legendary islands in the Atlantic; some show Atlantis and others show Antilla (or Antilia), a somewhat similar name. But a Buache map (1737) of the Atlantic between the Canary Islands and South America purports to show certain oceanic banks, located over the Mid-Atlantic Ridge on which many islands (most of them now gone) break the surface. As Charles Hapgood asks (*Maps of the Ancient Sea Kings:* 1966): "Who in the year 1737 knew anything about the bottom of the Atlantic?" Nobody, perhaps, in 1737—but certainly somebody did in an earlier age when he originally made the map from which Buache got his information.

These messages from remote antiquity constitute a direct link between the present and the almost forgotten past. Their survival aided and encouraged the exploration of the ocean and pointed the way to the discovery of Plato's "opposite continent" on the other side of the "true ocean."

These copies of very ancient maps with indications of exact coastlines beneath the Antarctic ice, showing islands once over and now under the sea, sunken coasts and vanished land bridges, furnish us with a form of iconographic corroboration of the presence of civilized man prior to a general planetary upheaval. This catastrophe, involving a great rising of the waters, echoes of which exist in all legends and traditions of mankind, brought about considerable changes in the land areas of the world and destroyed a civilization.

The expertise of these original map makers may have aided some groups of a doomed civilization to escape the catastrophe that ended their world, enabling them to survive by successfully navigating giant ships through tsunami-like waves, finally to reach sanctuary on high lands and to begin a new ascent to civilization. This possibility has been immortalized in a tradition common to all races and peoples of the earth.

9

The Drowning
of a World

Although all races preserve a tradition of a Great
Flood, it is within the area of the peoples who lived
around the Atlantic circle, the Mediterranean, and in
the area of the Fertile Crescent that the legends most
resemble each other. This common tradition is closely
related to the destruction of Atlantis, the center of
civilization before the flood. Biblical and other ancient
traditions specify that the earlier inhabitants of the
world were destroyed by divine justice for their iniqui-
ties in order to provide an opportunity for a renewal of
mankind and a betterment of his imperfect nature. (It
is noteworthy that Plato reported that the Atlanteans
were struck down by catastrophe even while they
were engaged in a war of world conquest.)

The punishment of Atlantis, or the world before the
flood, and the annihilation of all its inhabitants except
for a selected few, has been a central theme of this
great tradition. In almost every legend a single man
and woman—with or without their immediate family
or followers—are spared, often with livestock or even
a bestiary of animals to repopulate the earth with
human beings *and* with animals.

In considering a global disaster characterized by
flooding as well as by earthquakes and volcanic eruptions the question arises as to where the covering

waters went after the flood. The flood, as evidently
seen and remembered, involved not only a constant
downpouring of rain lasting for many weeks but great
tidal waves that covered the islands, coasts, and low-
lands of the world. Undoubtedly the increase in sea
level did not come only from the rain but from another
source as well, the rapid melting of the Third Glaciation. The Old Testament (Genesis, Chapter 7:11) aptly
describes the dual nature of the flooding: "The same
day were all the fountains of the great deep broken up,
and the windows of heaven were opened."

When the earth became more tranquil the waters
receded in some places but remained at a higher level
of 500 to 600 feet or more in some places because of
seismic shifting. It is logical to assume that the greater
part of Atlantis remained drowned with only its mountain tops, now the Atlantic islands, still protruding
from the ocean. The former continent or large island
situated on the Atlantic Ridge fracture zone, one of the
most seismically disturbed areas of the planet, became
a permanent victim of the world catastrophe, although
in a future upheaval of the earth it might, for basically
the same reasons that it sank, be thrust up again to the
surface, just as Edgar Cayce and others have foretold.

The flood, the constant rain, and the earthquakes
which continued to shake the world were a convincing
manifestation to those still alive that the world was
ending. When the world had settled down again one
might well imagine that the descendants of the few
survivors, in the case of each tribe or area, subsequently claimed as an ancestor some commanding or
heroic figure who actually existed and had, with divine
help, escaped the flood and led the way to survival.

The flood legends that have come down to us from
antiquity are a convincing indication that the human
race in all parts of the world remembered a time of
great flooding and destruction. In almost all the traditions God, or a special god among other dieties, de-
sired to destroy all but a few of the human race—and

start all over again. The sins of man varied but slightly among the legends (it would be natural for the survivors of a catastrophe to attempt to ascribe an understandable reason for the annihilation of their race). The reasons are usually explained by man having become too proud and therefore no longer obedient to the Divine Will; too corrupt or too violent and also, in the cogent words of the Bible: "every imagination of the thoughts of his heart was only evil continually."

An examination of a variety of the legends of the races and nations of antiquity are interesting in their similarities and even in their local differences. Evidently a small number of survivors recounted the story and eventually caused it to be recorded in writing, with modifications stemming from their own particular cultures. Sometimes, in reading the fuller accounts from which the following information has been taken, we feel that we are hearing from eye witnesses of a disaster that drowned a world.

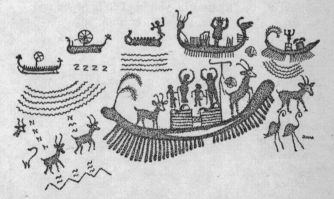

Cave drawings and incised carvings of ships from prehistoric times may be an early recollection of the Great Flood by its survivors. These ancient drawings, although from points as widely separated as Egypt, Sumeria, Spain, California, Scandinavia, and Central Europe, demonstrate a startling similarity. The last and largest one, apparently dealing with the loading and transport of animals, is reminiscent of Noah's Ark.

SOURCE	SURVIVORS	MEANS OF SURVIVAL
The Bible and the Torah	Noah, family animals, birds; "of clean beasts 7; others 2 each male and female."	Ark—300 cubits long x 50 wide x 30 high, made of gopher wood sealed with pitch.
Sumerian and Babylonian records	Xisuthros (or) Khasistratra, with family, friends, animals, and birds.	A vessel 5 stadia long and 5 broad.
Assyrian-Babylonian records	Ubaratutu (or) Khasisatra, with family, servants, cattle and wild beasts.	Vessel 600 cubits long and 60 in height and breadth.
Sumerian, Assyrian, Babylonian records from the library of King Ashur-banipal. (A variant of the preceding legend.)	Ut-napishtim, his family, and animals.	A vessel with "the seed of life on board."

CATASTROPHE	SALVATION
Rain for 40 days and 40 nights. "The waters prevailed . . . 150 days . . . The fountains of the great deep were broken up. . . . The waters covered the earth and the mountains, all that was in the dry land died. . . ."	The Ark landed upon the mountains of Ararat. Noah sent forth a raven and a dove. The dove did not return from its third flight. Noah then left the Ark.
"A terrible water spout rose to the sky, the ocean overflowed the shore, and the rivers their banks."	The Gordyene mountains of Armenia. Survivors returned to Sippara to dig up records of civilization.
Duration 6 days and 6 nights. "Tidal seas and water spouts. . . . The corpses of the drowned floated like seaweed . . ."	Mount Nizar. The dove returned but not the raven. "Khasisatra and his wife henceforward were granted to live like gods . . ."
Deluge lasted 6 days and 6 nights. "On the seventh day Ut-napishtim looked out—everything was silent—mankind had gone back to mud . . ."	The ship ran aground at Mount Nizar. Ut-napishtim loosed a dove, a swallow, and a raven. The raven stayed to eat the corpses. No bird returned. After debarking and a debate between the gods, immortality was bestowed on the survivors.

SOURCE	SURVIVORS	MEANS OF SURVIVAL
Greek tradition and ancient commentaries	Deukalion, his wife Pyrrha, children, and terrestrial animals, including pigs, horses, lions, and serpents.	A great coffer.
Satapatha Brahmana and the Mahabharata of India	Manu (variant: Manu and seven others— the Rishi).	A fish that Manu caught and spared grew larger and larger and told Manu to build a ship and attach it to the fish's horn. (The fish is generally considered to be an avatar of Vishnu.)
The Puranas, India	Satyrawata.	A vessel directed by the Divine Fish.
Persian tradition	Yima and a thousand couples, plus animals and birds.	"A *vara* (underground fortress or tomb) made of clay, a horserun long, stocked with food, fruits, plants and animals, but no evil people, persons with uneven teeth, or lepers . . ." The *vara* was "3 stories deep with wide avenues . . ."

CATASTROPHE	SALVATION
Deluge lasted 9 days and nights "with water issuing from the earth and the sea overflowing . . ."	Mount Parnassus. A chasm later opened in the earth at Bambyce and the waters drained through it. Deukalion and Pyrrha threw stones into a field which became men and women according to the sex of each thrower.
Deluge.	The divine fish pulled the ship over the mountains of the north to Mount Himavat. After landing Manu re-created all living things himself or, in variant, Manu was granted a young woman and then repeopled the earth.
Flood lasted 7 days and "the three wells were submerged . . ."	The fish brought the vessel to land.
Earthquakes, floods, and fires destroyed the world.	Yima and his friends came to the surface and rebuilt the world.

SOURCE	SURVIVORS	MEANS OF SURVIVAL
The Koran	Noah, his family, and animals.	Ark.
Welsh legend, "The Third Catastrophe of Britain"	Dwyfan and Dwyfach.	Vessel without rigging.
Norse Edda	Bergalmer and wife.	A large vessel.
Lithuanian tradition	Some couples of human beings and of animals.	A high mountain and a shell.
Pre-Christian Irish legends	Queen Ceseair and her court.	A ship.

CATASTROPHE	SALVATION
A flood that covered the earth. "The earth's surface seethed . . . The ark moved amid waves like mountains. . . ."	Allah said: "O Earth, swallow up the waters and thou, O Heaven, withhold thy rain." They landed on Mount Djudi.
A great flood caused by the eruption of Llynllion— The Lake of the Waves.	After the waters subsided Dwyfan and Dwyfach repeopled Britain.
Flood and fire. "The waters rose, the earth became dark, the ocean serpents beat the water. The stony hills dashed together. Earth sank into the ocean. The bright stars fell from heaven. The fire rose up to heaven itself. . ."	When water subsided Bergalmer and his wife repeopled the earth.
Flood and wind which lasted 12 days and nights.	When waters reached the highest mountain and were about to engulf the people, the Supreme Being, who was eating giant nuts at the time, dropped a shell which they climbed into and sailed to dry land.
Flooding waters of the ocean.	They sailed for 7½ years but never got back to Ireland which, washed over by the ocean, was uninhabitable for 200 years after the Deluge.

SOURCE	SURVIVORS	MEANS OF SURVIVAL
Chinese legend	Yao and 7 others (or) Fa Li, wife and children.	A sailing junk.
Aztec-Toltec records	Coxcox (or) Tezpi (or) Teocipactli, with wife, children, and animals.	Large raft made of cypress wood.
Aztec-Toltec Chichimec records—considered the fourth catastrophic age of the world—the Water Age, or "Sun."	Coxcox and wife, Xochi-quetzal.	Hollowed tree trunk.

CATASTROPHE	SALVATION
Flood and earthquake. "The pillars of Heaven were broken. . . . The earth fell to pieces . . . The waters burst forth and overflowed it. . . . The system of the Universe was totally disordered. . . ."	The waters receded or (variant) "The slashed trunk of the gushing Tree of Heaven was repaired by a goddess."
A flood that covered the earth for 52 years.	Coxcox sent out vultures and other birds to look for land. The vultures found carcasses to eat and did not return. Finally, a hummingbird returned with a leaf and Coxcox landed on the crooked mountain of Colhuacan.
The flood covered the earth for 52 years. "The mountains sank beneath the water. All mankind drowned or changed into fish."	A divine bird guided the raft to an emerging mountain.

SOURCE	SURVIVORS	MEANS OF SURVIVAL
Maya re-cords—the *Popul Vuh* and the *Book of Chilam Balaam*	A few people.	Deep caves.
Toltec records	Seven friends with their wives.	A great chest.
Chibcha tribal legend—South America	Bochica and his wife.	They escaped to the highest mountain by riding on "camels."
Huron tribal legend—North America	The Great Father of the Indian Tribes, with wife, family, and animals.	A large raft.

CATASTROPHE	SALVATION
Flood, fire, and earthquakes. "A great noise was heard in the sky and heavy rain fell from the sky by night and day. Men tried to climb the houses but the houses submerged. The sky fell down . . . the dry land sank, and in a moment the great annihilation was finished. . . ."	When the catastrophe ended the survivors came out of the caves.
An all-enveloping flood covered the earth. The waters attained a depth of 15 *caxtolmolatli* over the highest mountains.	When the flood stopped the survivors and their descendents wandered for 104 years. When they finally settled in Mexico they built a high tower to escape from future floods.
Flood.	After the flood ceased Bochica opened a hole in the earth at Tequendama to drain off the waters.
A world flood lasting several months.	During this time the animals on the raft constantly complained and became unruly. When the raft landed on the emerging earth the animals were punished by having power of speech taken from them.

SOURCE	SURVIVORS	MEANS OF SURVIVAL
Mandal tribal legend—North America	Numoch-mochbah, a white man.	A huge covered canoe.
Dakota Sioux and also Chickasaw tribal legends—North America	Some survivors (or) 1 family and 2 animals of every kind.	Very big canoes.
Hopi tribal legends—North America. The Destruction of the Third World—the one before the present.	Members of the Hopi tribe.	They fastened themselves into tall plants with hollow stems.

CATASTROPHE	SALVATION
A flood which covered Numochmochbah's home-land in the East.	When the waters receded new land was found in the West where Numochmoch-bah stayed. He found people there who had hidden in tunnels and had sent out a mouse to see if the flood was over.
A flood of many weeks' duration.	Dry land was found in the West when the flood ended.
Flood. "The waters were loosened upon the earth. Waves higher than moun-tains rolled in on the land. The continents broke asunder and sank beneath the waves."	When the flood stopped survivors found themselves on top of one of the highest mountains. Everything else was water. At the bottom of the sea lay all the proud cities, the *patuwvotas* (airships) and the worldly treasures corrupted with evil. A new world was created and the people were admonished by the Legate of the Creator to carry out the plan of creation or the new Fourth World would be destroyed as well.

SOURCE	SURVIVORS	MEANS OF SURVIVAL
Guarani tribal legends—South America	Tamandere and wife.	A giant palm tree with a supply of fruit.
Inca tradition—South America	A few people (or) one person.	The highest mountains of the Andes.
Tuscarora tribal legend—Brazil	Twins—Tamandere and Aricute (whose quarreling brought on the flood) and their wives.	A high tree on a mountaintop.
Arctic Eskimo Legend	A few Eskimos with their families.	Many kayaks lashed together.

CATASTROPHE	SALVATION
A great flood. "The palm tree became uprooted and floated over the flood. All those who remained in the valleys drowned. The flood continued until the waters reached the sky."	Tamandere heard the beating of wings of a heavenly bird and soon the flood receded.
Flood for 60 days and nights. A llama staring sadly at the sky told his owner that the sea would cover the earth. The llama led his owner to the top of Mount Villcacoto where people, birds, and animals had congregated.	When the flood ceased the surviving people, llamas, and wild animals descended from the high Andes and repopulated the earth.
A deluge which submerged the whole earth.	When the waters seemed to recede one twin gave his wife a fruit to drop in order to estimate the water level from the splash. She kept dropping fruit until one hit dry earth. The twins descended from the tree but at once resumed their fighting.
A great rising flood accompanied by an icy wind.	The flood ceased when a sorcerer threw his arrow and earrings into the sea, shouting: "Wind, enough!" The waters calmed down and receded.

SOURCE	SURVIVORS	MEANS OF SURVIVAL
Tlingit tribal legend— Alaska	Members of Tlingit tribe.	Great canoes.

A flood legend of ancient Egypt is a curious one since it implies that the Great Flood was simply one of a series of disasters. This is reminiscent of the statement, as reported by Plato, made by the Egyptian priests of Saïs to Solon: "There have been and there will be again, many destructions of mankind arising out of many causes."

One of the greatest of these destructions, as remembered by the priests of Egypt, was a flood which came at the end of the rule of the God Kings who reigned "before the flood" and prior to the first historic dynasty of Egypt. According to legend, Ra, the Sun God, wishing to punish mankind, caused a flood which drowned great sections of the earth. He then relented and promised the remaining Egyptians as a future recompense (certainly the most unusual reward ever promised to the survivors of a flood) to send them a flood *every year*. The future floods, however, would be more moderate and more welcome as they would continue to make the Nile Delta constantly more fertile.

The Great Pyramid of Gizeh was said to have been constructed shortly before or after the flood, not as a tomb but as a permanent and indestructible storehouse

CATASTROPHE	SALVATION
A flood.	Tribe took to the rising sea in great canoes. Bears and wolves tried to climb aboard but were beaten off. Canoes washed up to top of highest peak. From the mountaintop Tlingits watched trees, animals, and people flow past in rapid current.

of knowledge that was literally built into its dimensions and orientation. The pyramid of Cholula, in Mexico, was also, according to Aztec legend, built as a refuge against future floods.

It is intriguing to note the absence of a general flood legend in one of the cultures of antiquity, that of the far sailing Phoenician and Carthaginian explorers of the ocean, seafarers who would certainly have been the ones to be most familiar with the sinking or flooding of land areas in the Atlantic. Perhaps this may be explained by the disappearance of the original Phoenician and Carthaginian records which were either destroyed or later combined in the surprisingly accurate portolano charts. There may also be an element of ancient censorship in this apparent mystery as the Phoenician and Carthaginian seafarers, anxious to keep their profitable trade routes secret, had decreed a mandatory death penalty for all crews of foreign ships they encountered in the Atlantic, as well as for their own crews if they spoke of the Atlantic routes in foreign ports. They also spread the rumor that, since the catastrophe, the Atlantic was not only unnavigable but contained dangerous mud shoals, filled with seaweed which held back the ships, and fierce sea monsters, a discouraging outlook which evidently did not keep Carthaginian pilots from sailing across the Atlantic to North and South America, where their artifacts are still being discovered. In a word, it is probable that the Phoenico-Carthaginians, being more familiar through their voyages than were other races with the basis of the flood legend, kept it quiet and turned it to their own advantage, and profit.

Other flood legends of the Americas, Africa, and the islands of the Pacific Ocean differ considerably in some details, especially those of animal participation and, in some more primitive tribes, of animal responsibility for the deluge. But they testify to the memory of all races that, at some time in the far past, a global catastrophe involving a flood occurred and left a memory that, through all the intervening generations, has never quite vanished.

The earth remembers it too. In various areas throughout the world layered strata showing flood levels, shorelines dropped underwater or forced upward, caves above and below the sea and the stalactite and stalagmite evidence therein, gravel bars and giant scours in river systems, remains of marine life in deserts and in high mountain ranges are a reminder of a sudden local disaster of flood and upheaval.

A convincing indication of the suddenness of a world flood is still observable in the condition of animal remains within the Arctic regions where millions of animals were, within a relatively recent geological period, suddenly killed and "quick frozen" into the mud and ice of the permafrost. It is as if hordes of grazing or hunting animals, swept by sudden and enormous tidal waves, were washed like flotsam at the edge of a tide and left in masses in a continent-wide tidal line extending through northern Canada, Alaska, and Siberia. They are still there by the million, evident as masses of bones and often as flesh and fur, frequently disinterred from the permafrost by construction or mining operations.

Dr. Frank Hibbon, Professor of Archaeology at the University of New Mexico, who visited the area on an expedition to study Alaska mammoths, observed, regarding the pellmell mixture of the frozen remains of horses, bison, saber-tooth tigers, lions, deer, bears, and mammoths:

> Within the mass, frozen solid, lie the twisted parts of animals and trees intermingled with lenses of ice and layers of peat and mosses. It looks as though in the middle of some catastrophe of ten thousand years ago the whole Alaskan world of living animals and plants was suddenly frozen in mid-motion . . . dumped in all attitudes of death. . . . Legs and torsos and heads and fragments were found together in piles or scattered separately . . . animals (were) torn apart and scattered over the landscape even though they may have weighed several tons . . .

Dr. Hibbon also suggested an explanation especially pertinent to the ancient legend:

> . . . violent storms might explain the peculiar finds of so many animals crammed in cavern fissures from different geological periods . . .

Siberia contains islands off the coast of the Arctic Ocean, including Liakoff which, among others, seems to be almost entirely composed of tusks and bones of great mammals, surrounded by underwater ledges composed of still more bones; evidently this was where the high point of the death tide deposited them. In caves and hilltops of Central Europe, boneyards of many different species of animals—rhinoceros, horses, lions, deer, aurochs, wolves, all massed together, show the immediacy of danger and a futile attempt at survival.

Immanuel Velikovsky *(Earth in Upheaval* and *Worlds in Collision),* attributing the global disaster to particular causes, such as the effects of the wanderings of Venus, points out the worldwide aspect of the catastrophe:

> In many places on the earth—on all continents—bones of sea animals and polar land animals and tropical animals have been found in great melees; so also in the Cumberland Cave in Maryland, in the Chou Kou Tien fissures in China, and in Germany and Denmark. Hippopotamuses and ostriches were found together with seals and reindeer . . . from the Arctic to the Antarctic . . . in the high mountains and in the deep seas we find innumerable signs of great upheavals, ancient and recent . . ."

The ubiquity of a prehistoric disaster and the seeming inexplicable disappearance of whole species was remarked upon by Charles Darwin as a result of his zoological investigations related to *The Origin of Species*. Darwin wrote:

> The mind . . . is irresistibly hurried into the belief of some great catastrophe, but thus to destroy animals, both large and small, in southern Patagonia, in Brazil, on the Cordillera of Peru, in North America up to Bering Strait, *we must shake the entire framework of the globe*.

As we can imagine from the frozen or skeleton remains from the great animal hecatombs the sudden doom that overwhelmed them when the earth shook and the waters rose, it is also possible to imagine a sequence of events when the civilization which existed before the Flood came to a sudden end. We can do this through the interpretation of the descriptive traditions and incomplete legends which have reached us across the gulf of time as well as from the probable reactions of human beings whose nature, whatever modification may have taken place in the land masses and seas of the earth, has not perceptibly changed.

> It is probable that over a period of years there had been warnings from the colleges of the astrologers and from the priests in their temple courts of Atlantis that the tremendous explosions carried on by scientists in regions of the north would either cause the anger of heaven or destroy the balance of the earth in relation to the stars and planets. Individual scholars, studying ancient records, had predicted that the explosive shocks might loose the inner fires of the earth with disastrous results. Despite these warnings the experiments were continued to develop weapons as a means of easy and final conquest over armies raised against the empire's spreading dominance over the other continents, and also as a tool to rid whole areas of troublesome animals, larger and more dangerous than those of a later day. Observers in the north had reported great turbulence in the ice-covered northern seas, an increasing shifting and opening of the ice fields and there had been worldwide smoking and eruptions of volcanoes and a rising of the coastal tides and a restlessness in the earth, with shocks now being felt in the central island itself.
>
> We can imagine that some of the great transport ships had already put to sea carrying a variety of people, their tools, plants, animals, and records to other parts of the empire on the mainland, over an increasingly turbulent sea.

The last hours of Atlantis (or whatever name was used by the civilization before the flood) has been imaginatively described by Frederick H. Martens (*The Romance of Evolution*) in an account which, however fanciful, is based on existing legends as well as geological indications. He describes the indifference of the populace to the warnings of the priests and the astrologers whose predictions of disaster over the years had not come true. The people in the world to be destroyed were, as dwellers in doomed lands have always been, persistently optimistic.

What if red stars drop from the skies? What if volcanoes smoke? Stars have fallen and volcanoes smoked before—and nothing has come of it. What if the fleets have put out from port, and the kings and their harems and household left for the African coast? . . .

The population of the great metropolis of Atlantis, the City of the Golden Gates, is more concerned about the day's festival in the arena.

The fairest and most skillful of all the women bullkillers, a big blond woman from Gaul, is billed for the bullfight this afternoon! Tomorrow will be time enough to think of flight!

The streets are filled with people, laughing, jostling, talking. Mingled with the Atlantides are traders from distant lands: Scandinavians, Gauls, men from the lake villages, oily traders from Tyre, Babylon, and even Nineveh, though it is as yet but a small town. There are men from Asia, there are men from Africa, and no one gives a thought to danger as the golden afternoon declines.

The great inner port of Atlantis is still crowded with ships, and the hard, weather-beaten old sea dogs laugh all of the priests' warnings to scorn . . . they do not trust a landsman's knowledge in anything.

They are contemptuous of the warnings. A leader among them raises a great flagon of wine and waves toward the volcano smoking to the west of the great wall. "Tidal waves, water spouts? We may have a little rough weather, but nothing more. . . . The whole College of Priests could not make me believe anything else!" As he stands there the rays of the setting sun glistening and sparkling on the silver inlays of his heavy green glass drinking cup, a chorus of sailor voices rings out from the tavern behind him.

But even while the sailors sing their songs the gold of the sky pales into spectral gray. Minute by minute this pallor darkens into purple blackness, while from the sea sweeps a vast wind, with a high, curious moaning sound! A sudden silence has fallen on all the thousands of living human beings—the song is hushed, and laughter, cries and chatter along the squares and wharf-fronts have died away. The moaning voice of the wind rises higher and higher, to a shrill, whining, hysterical note. And then—without warning, comes the crash of the bursting volcanoes! High columns of burning lava and blinding flame shoot mile-high into the skies, and in a moment the streets of Atlantis are filled with a panic-stricken mob. Men, women and children flee shrieking into the great temples, into the great halls and barracks that front the squares, to escape the glowing, tingling lava-ash, and the black rain of soot which covers the bronze-gold walls and the white marble of the palaces like a pall. But even while gray-black torrents of molten lava are rolling down from the surrounding mountains on the city, comes a new terror.

The tall guards, cased in bronze armor from head to foot, are pushing back the men and women who try to break into the palace entrance with their oak lance-shafts. The kings and their household have fled. The palaces are empty. Their treasures are lumbering through the African forests in cart and on camel back. But—an order is an order! The captain of the guard, when he left in haste with the body of his men, forgot to relieve these sentinels. And so they still stand off the frantic crowd with their lance-shafts, and defend the entrance to the empty palace while their whole world is falling to pieces around them!

Now, with a tremendous shock, the first earthquake-wave tears apart the great city across its middle! For a moment a vast, terrible abyss opens before thousands of eyes which will never see another sun! In the very bowels of the earth, miles down, as the surface of the earth is torn apart, gleams a great wonderful and hideous rose of fire, and a hot gust so terrible goes up from it that thousands, breathing in the flame which trembles invisible in the air, fall into the great rose-gleaming fire-pit like singed flies. But the fire-rose of Earth's heart is seen but for a moment! Another fearsome shock and, while palaces and temples crumble on every side, the waters of the Atlantic rush into the gap that splits the island in half—rush in and over. For now, slowly, quietly, calmly, after the two terrific upheavals, like some great flat stone which . . . moves in strange circles down into unknown deeps, *the whole great island of Atlantis sinks—thousands of feet—beneath the waves!*

Fifteen minutes before the sailors were singing . . . the world was bright. Birds trilled, men laughed and talked. *Ten minutes before* the palace guards were still calling "Fall back!" to the mob surging against their crossed lance-shafts. *Five minutes before*—the air and sky were still as death. Not a living soul survived on Atlantis. There was no sound in the air for some moments. Only, had there been eyes to see so vast and wonderful a thing, the entire island of Atlantis was drawing its curious descending circles beneath the waves, like a great flat stone, as it moved slowly on down to its final resting-place on the Atlantic bottom, where it lies today . . .

Some of the ships that had already sailed from port before the catastrophe occurred continued on their way, through mountainous seas and storms so intense that many of them foundered at sea. When the surviving ships reached the coasts they were aiming for they found that the coasts themselves had receded. The ships were swept over alluvial plains and flatlands, now become seas, until some of them grounded on high plateaus and others were swept up the sides of mountains. When the earthquakes and flooding subsided, the survivors descended from the high places where their ships had been washed to establish what they had been able to save of their civilization in the new and savage world which developed into the world of known history.

This persistent legend of a continuum of civilization despite catastrophe would, of course, be more believable if there were some tangible and definite proof of such transmittal and also, apart from legend, if some other proof of an organized human escape from a worldwide disaster could be found. One may still exist in an almost inaccessible region, known to mankind for thousands of years, assailed by scientific disbelief but sustained by faith, so persistent that it has attained an independent existence whether or not the relic corporeally exists where man has thought it to lie for thousands of years. It may be but one of the survival ships of the world that was. It is called Noah's Ark.

10

The Impossible Artifact from the Great Flood

The memory of the Flood and of a survival ark is perhaps the most persistent of man's legends, if legend it be. It occupies, in the King James version of the Bible, five chapters of the Book of Genesis, while the creation of the world, the story of Adam, the sending forth from the Garden of Eden, and the crime of Cain occupy only four chapters.

The Biblical record of the Ark coming to rest "upon the mountains of Ararat" has been generally accepted by the Christian world for almost two millenia, and by other preceding cultures including, among others, the Hebrew, Armenian, Syrian, and Mesopotamian, centuries before that. The Islamic world has believed the Ark legend for almost 1,400 years. With such a concentration of belief it is natural that present-day explorers have, especially during the last hundred years, exercised great efforts on ascertaining whether a huge ship does lie externally fixed on Ararat. They have been encouraged both by reports of persons who have climbed the mountain and claim to have seen, touched, and entered the Ark and, fairly recently, by reports of pilots who claim to have seen it while flying near the top of Ararat and even by photographs taken by space satellite, an interesting verification of an artifact from the earliest civilization by an artifact of the most recent.

Because of the persistence of the belief in the Ark on Ararat not only among religious groups but also on the part of some students of prehistory (who feel that if it is not Noah's Ark something very much resembling a ship is resting high on Mount Ararat) the question of its possible existence has been put to well-established archaeologists. The answer given by Frolich Rainey, Director of the University of Pennsylvania Museum is short, witty, and to the point:

Absolutely anything is possible in this world, but if there's anything that's *impossible* in archaeology, this is it.

But is it really so impossible for an ancient ship to be frozen and thereby preserved on the side of a mountain? It might be observed that the question of location and climate raised by skeptics might tend to authenticate the report and that the only way for a wooden ship or a giant wooden artifact to be preserved for millennia would be for it to be buried under ice, under frozen mud, deep inside a cavern, on the ocean bottom in deep waters, or under the desert sands. That such a ship might be washed up the side of a mountain and be frozen there under a glacier would be the result of a major disturbance of the earth, which sent oceans and seas in great careening floods over the shaking, rising and falling surface of the world. But for an archaeologist to consider the probability of a ship on the mountain he would first have to admit the possibility of a disaster of flood and earthquake within human memory, even if the latter concept is not accepted by the majority of the archaeological establishment.

Commentators of antiquity and the Middle Ages referred to the Ark on Ararat (from an ancient word for Armenia—Urartu) in a generally informative way, taking its presence there for granted especially since it could then still be seen by anyone who climbed high enough up the mountain or even, at some times, be seen from the plain, black against the glacial ice and snow. A Babylonian priestly writer of 300 B.C., Berossus, mentioned that people who climbed up to the Ark were accustomed to scrape pitch from its sides for use as amulets. Other writers recounted that relic seekers took not only pitch, but also pieces of wood from the Ark without noticeably diminishing it, since the climb was difficult and the Ark frequently covered by snow.

Epiphanius of Salamis, in the fourth century A.D., used the Ark's tangible presence as a proof of doctrine when he wrote:

> Do you seriously suppose that we were unable to prove our point when even to this day the remains of Noah's Ark are shown in the country of the Kurds?

This 1,500-year-old reference to the Kurds is especially interesting as the Kurds, known for their propensity in modern times for shooting at strangers, represent one of the many perils which act as a deterrent to the explorers of Ararat. Other animate perils include wild dog packs, wolves, snakes, and bears. Among the principal inanimate perils are avalanches, rock falls, the snow and ice of the glacier, suddenly opening cavities in the ice and frequent earthquakes.

Flavius Josephus, a Jewish historian of the second century, was another early writer who also treated the Ark with a certain matter-of-fact acceptance and scholastically observed that the name of a town near the mountain, Nakhichevan, means "the landing place" in Armenian, adding: ". . . for it is there that the Ark came to land . . . the Armenians . . . show relics of it to this day."

Marco Polo, the tireless Venetian traveler who has left us a valuable step-by-step account of his travels through medieval Asia, made a thoughtful observation when he passed through Armenia in the thirteenth century:

> And you should know that in this land of Armenia, the Ark of Noah still rests on the top of a certain great mountain where the snow stays so long that no one can climb it. The snow never melts—it gets thicker every snowfall . . .

Marco Polo, with commendable geographic and meteorological acumen, foresaw what would make the persistently reported Ark on Mount Ararat difficult to reach and explore. Parts of the glacier are now 100 to 140 feet thick, and the ship could be under this ice or sunk into a huge crevasse. The occasional reported sightings in modern times, usually from the air, have generally been during dry spells which have melted the ice, or seismic shiftings of the mountain itself.

For hundreds of generations travelers at the foot of Mount Ararat have strained their eyes in an attempt to discover anything that looked like a giant ship protruding from the glacier or visible on the saddle between the two "Mountains of Ararat," the conelike lesser Ararat and the central, domelike Ararat. Jehan Haithon, a reputed Armenian prince who became a French monk, observed in the thirteenth century:

> On the mountain [Ararat] at the summit, a great black object is always visible . . . said to be the Ark of Noah . . .

In this connection one must remember that often our eyes tend to see what we expect to see and any outcropping of rock or crevasse in the ice might temporarily take on the form of a ship, thereby satisfying the faith of the viewer as well as his confidence in his own clarity of vision.

In the nineteenth century, however, when the

mountain was successfully climbed, the Ark was not found. Earthquakes had changed the terrain from time to time, destroying the St. James monastery where relics of the Ark had been kept. (A fault runs through the area.) One earthquake in May of 1883 opened up a section of the mountain and exposed a wooden ship to the view of Turkish commissioners who visited the area to assess the earthquake damage. The commissioners reported finding a huge dark wooden mass protruding from a glacier, estimating that it was forty to fifty feet high but of unknown length as the rest of it was embedded far back in the glacier. The commission, which included an English member, entered into the interior, part of which seemed to be partitioned off into a series of compartments up to fifteen feet high. They were of the opinion, from the way the supposed ship lay, that it had slid down the mountain with the glacier. Faced with this frozen vessel in the mountain the commission reported that Noah's Ark had been found.

Newspapers in the United States reacted in the somewhat jocular vein of the type now reserved for UFO reports. The New York *Herald* suggested that if the Ark was so full of ice part of the cost of shipping it to America could be defrayed by the sale of ice during the coming summer. The same paper added in another editorial a timeless criticism of the U.S. Navy, writing that "the Navy Department ought to purchase the Ark at once since the world's greatest republic ought to have at least one ship that will not rot as soon as it leaves a Navy yard."

While the excitement about finding the Ark was still continuing, a Prince Nouri of Mesopotamia appeared at the Chicago World's Fair of 1893 and made an offer to a group of financiers that he would, after receiving appropriate backing, bring the Ark back to the World's Fair.

But whatever was found on the mountain was soon covered again by ice and it was not until the two World

Wars that a shiplike object was seen and photographed over and under the ice by pilots flying over Mount Ararat.

During the last months of the Romanov dynasty of Russia reports were current on the Caucasian front that an aviator had found a large ship on a half frozen lake on Mount Ararat and that as a result an Imperial investigation was ordered. The Tsar was reported to be especially interested in the project on religious grounds and measurements and photographs were taken of the object although the results of the investigation were hidden, lost, or destroyed during the Russian Revolution, which happened shortly after.

An American version of the incident appeared in the *New Eden,* a Los Angeles magazine, in 1940. It was attributed to "Lieutenant Vladimir Roskovitsky," a pilot in the Imperial Russian Airforce who was located at a base about twenty-five miles northwest of Mount Ararat in the late summer of 1916. The Lieutenant's mission on the day of the flight was to test a new supercharger at a relatively high altitude in a light plane. Part of this account follows:

. . . As I looked down at the great stone battlements surrounding the lower part of the mountain, I remembered having heard that it had never been climbed since the year 700 B.C., when some pilgrims were supposed to have gone up there to scrape some tar off an old shipwreck, to make good-luck emblems to wear around their necks and to prevent their crops being destroyed by excessive rainfall . . .

A couple of miles around the snow-capped dome, and then a long swift glide down the south side, and then we suddenly came upon a perfect frozen gem of a lake blue as a sapphire, but still frozen over on the shade side. We circled around, and returned for another look at it. Suddenly my companion whirled around and yelled something, and excitedly pointed down at the overflow end of the lake . . .

A submarine? No, it wasn't, for it had stubby masts, but the top was rounded over with only a flat cat-walk, about five feet across, down the length of it. What a strange craft, built as though the designer had expected the waves to roll over the top most of the time, and had engineered it to wallow in the sea like a log, with those stubby masts carrying enough sail to keep it facing the waves . . .

We flew down as close as safety permitted and took several circles around it. We were surprised when we got close to it, at the immense size of the thing, for it was as long as a city block, and would compare very favorably in size to the modern battleships of today. It was grounded on the shore of the lake, with one-fourth under water. It had been partly dismantled on one side near the front, and on the other side there was a great doorway nearly twenty feet square, but with the other door gone. This seemed quite out of proportion, as even today, ships seldom have doors even half that large.

After seeing all we could from the air, we broke all speed records down to the airport . . .

The Captain asked us several questions, and ended by saying, "Take me up there; I want to look at it." We made the trip without incident and returned to the airport.

"What do you make of it?" I asked, as we climbed out of the plane.

"Astounding!" he replied. "Do you know what that ship is? . . .

"This strange craft," explained the Captain, "is Noah's Ark. It has been sitting up there for nearly five thousand years. Being frozen up for nine or ten months of the year, it couldn't rot, and has been in cold storage, as it were, all this time. You have made the most amazing discovery . . ."

When the Captain sent this report to the Russian Government, it aroused considerable interest, and the Czar sent two special companies of soldiers to climb the mountain. One group of fifty men attacked one side, and the other group of one hundred men attacked the big mountain from the other side. Two weeks of hard work were required to chop out a trail along the cliffs of the lower part of the mountain, and it was nearly a month before the Ark was reached.

Complete measurements were taken, and plans drawn of it, as well as many photographs, all of which were sent to the Czar of Russia.

The Ark was found to contain hundreds of small rooms, and some rooms were very large, with high ceilings. The unusually large rooms had a fence of great timbers across them, some of which were two feet thick, as if designed to hold beasts ten times the size of elephants. Other rooms also were lined with tiers of cages, somewhat like one sees today at a poultry show, only instead of chicken wire, they had rows of tiny iron bars along the front.

Everything was heavily painted with a wax-like paint resembling shellac, and the workmanship of the craft showed all the signs of a high type of civilization. The wood used throughout was oleander, which belongs to the cypress family, and never rots; which of course, coupled with the fact of its being frozen most of the time, accounted for its perfect preservation.

The expedition found on the peak of the mountain above the ship the remains of the timbers which were missing out of one side of the ship. It seemed that these timbers had been hauled up to the top of the peak, and used to build a tiny one-room shrine . . . and it had either caught fire or been struck by lightning as the timbers were considerably burned and charred over, and the roof was completely burned off.

A few days after this expedition sent its report to the Czar, the Government was overthrown, and godless Bolsheviks took over, so that the records were never made public, and probably were destroyed in the zeal of the Bolsheviks to discredit all religion and belief in the truth of the Bible.

We White Russians of the Air Fleet escaped through
Armenia . . .

The veracity of the above report has long been held
in some doubt, since Roskovitsky was apparently not
the pilot's real name (it was probably altered for
reasons of personal security because of the violently
antireligious policy at that time). The names of two of
the pilots who saw the mysterious ship in the ice now
appear to have been First Lieutenants Zabolotsky and
Lesin of the Third Caucasian Air Detachment. It was
these and others who supplied the information later
made public under a pseudonym by Colonel Alexandr
Koor, who was in command of troops in the Ararat
sector in 1916.

The account is not unsupported, even considering
the confusion of the revolution and the ensuing civil
war in Russia. Other officers of the Imperial Army
have confirmed the discovery of a ship on Mount
Ararat in a declivity on the saddle between the two
Ararat peaks and the activities of the investigation
expedition. In addition, a detachment of five hundred
soldiers on a march around the northern part of Mount
Ararat in the summer of 1917 passed under an enormous barge on the slopes of the mountain. The barge
receded back into a glacier.

Russian interest in the Ark continued into World
War II, when Soviet Army Major J. Maskelyn, on duty
with the camouflage service, attempted to verify what
the imperial aviators had reported seeing in 1916.
Major Maskelyn sent a plane on a reconnaissance
flight over Mount Ararat and the pilot duly reported
sighting a large vessel half sunken in an icy lake, just
as had been reported a quarter of a century earlier.
Thereupon, according to Major Maskelyn, special in-
vestigators were sent to the spot and found that the
ship or barge was made of wood, now fossilized, and
was over 400 feet long. (One remembers the Biblical

length of 450 feet.) Nothing more was released about the vessel or its contents.

It may well be that the remains of the great ship lie on the side of Ararat facing Russia or Soviet Armenia, and this would explain the large number of photographs that Russian aviators reportedly have taken before, during, and after World War II. Many of these photographs were seen by American airmen during the fraternization period of World War II and have shown the alleged Ark in varying stages of emergence from

Position of the alleged Noah's Ark in a glacial lake as reported by Russian aviators in 1916. Subsequently it was seen before, during and after World War II by explorers, helicopter pilots and American airmen. According to general tradition and belief, the Ark only becomes visible during periods of extensive thaw and at such times has been visited by local mountaineers. The much photographed Ark "imprints" on page 201 may have been where the Ark once rested, leaving part of its structure, before it later slid to another part of the glacier. Recent reports suggest that the vessel has split into two parts or has been wholly or partially destroyed.

the ice, according to the weather or season in which the photographs were taken. But the Russian pilots, despite their friendliness, never gave any of these photographs to their then American allies.

American pilots, however, especially during Lend Lease flights in 1942, took a number of photographs on their own of various objects purporting to be the Ark, some of which have been published in the *Stars and Stripes* and other magazines. During wartime operations, however, pilots could only "sneak" a quick look at the area with little time available for locating the site. But some U.S. pilots obtained a good look at the vessel on the mountain fourteen years after World War II from an air base in Turkey.

One of these pilots was Second Lieutenant Gregor Schwinghammer, assigned to the 428th Tactical Flight Squadron (F-100s) based at Adana, Turkey, during the "Cold War." Lieutenant Schwinghammer's testimony has never before been published in any article or book* concerning the Ark. Gregor Schwinghammer spent twelve consecutive years as a pilot with the USAF and was separated in 1968 with the rank of Captain.

During the period he was interviewed by the author, the direct answers he gave to questions created the opinion that he was stating facts without exaggeration or embroidery but simply as he saw them. Captain Schwinghammer still employs his quick reflexes and keen vision as a chief pilot for a commercial airline. His testimony of what he saw from the F-100 over Mount Ararat is especially interesting because of the way it seems to mesh with previous reports.

Question: *Who first told you that it was possible to see Noah's Ark while you were in Turkey?*

---

* Although a number of books dealing with the Ark are mentioned in the bibliography of this book among the most recent and complete are *The Ark on Ararat*—Tim LaHaye, John Morris (1976); and *In Search of Noah's Ark*—Dave Balsiger and Charles E. Sellier Jr. (1976).

On our free time we got to know an American professor who told us about the ancient history of where we were. We used to take trips in a VW bus and look at ruins and then one of the Turkish pilots told us about the Ark. He was a liaison officer. Like the others he flew the C-47s which the Turks were using. We used to play poker with him and the town marshall. One day the pilot said to us, "Have you ever seen Noah's Ark?"
What was your reaction?

Our reaction was: "You've got to be kidding!" He said, "No, there's a sort of ship up on Mount Ararat. They say it's Noah's Ark." So we told him we wanted to see it and he took us up there several days later.
Was it hard to find?

No. It was easy for him. The only thing was that it was too near the Russian border, what with radar and all that, and besides, a C-130 had been shot down only two months before, so we were pretty nervous. There were three of us—two of us pilots with me as the wing man and the Turk sitting in tandem in back of the pilot. The Turk said, "We'll make one pass and have a look at it." We took a counter-clockwise swing around Mount Ararat and suddenly there it was, lying in the snow in a sort of saddle in the mountain.
What did it look like?

It looked like an enormous boxcar or a rectangular barge lying in a gulley. My first thought was, who would make a wooden building like a boat so high up on the mountain? When we made a quick pass over it at 4000-5000 feet I was able to see that it was banked, not as if it were a building, but like something that was movable but just stuck there.
How big was it?

The part I saw protruding from the snow and ice was about thirty to forty feet wide and about one hundred feet long before it went back into the snow. It was blackish in color. I heard later that the glacier kept slipping down the mountain and that was why it sometimes became exposed.

Did other Americans in the squadron see it later?

Everyone wanted to go and they took chances sneaking over it—of course, not all at the same time. I think everyone made at least one pass over it.

Did anyone take pictures of it?

Not that I know of. We were in too much of a hurry. I heard that the U-2 pilots got pictures of it, but we never saw any. The U-2 pilots used to stop in Adana but we didn't get to know them.

Do you believe that what you saw on Mount Ararat was really Noah's Ark?

All I know is that it was a great rectangular barge-type construction alone in the ice on a big desolate mountain. That is why it dazzled me.

In recent years a number of private expeditions have been organized to search the mountain and individuals have climbed on it as well, despite several deaths and

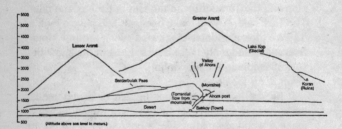

Schematic view of the two Ararats from the north. This side of the mountain is now especially difficult for foreign teams to explore, as it is visible to observers from across the Soviet border, who are apt to suspect spying missions. It has been surmised that the alleged Ark may have slid down this side of the mountain, either into the Valley of Ahora or into glacial Lake Kop. Fernand Navarra, a French searcher for the Ark, in the course of an exploratory climb from the Turkish side (see map below) in July 1955, found hewn wooden beams at the 13,700-foot level within an ice-filled crater near Lake Kop, with indications of more wood under the ice extending for hundreds of feet further. The frozen wooden beam, found in a treeless area, has been dated by carbon-14 tests, with some variations, to be several thousand years old.

disappearances. The town of Dogubayazit, at the foot of Mount Ararat, has long been a staging area for expeditions and individual climbers in search of the Ark. A French mountain climber, Fernand Navarra (*J'ai trouvé l'arche de Noë:* 1956) has brought back pieces of worked lumber beams tunneled from under the snow high on the mountain. A controlled carbon-14 test dated these at 5000 B.C. Armenians and Kurds have recounted their own visits to the alleged Ark during melting periods and one American pilot claimed to have flown over it and taken pictures from a helicopter. Another American, a manufacturer of helicopters, is interested in repeating the feat although, one might point out, American helicopters are now suspect near the Iranian and Russian borders of Turkey where Mount Ararat is located.

A British expedition organized by the distinguished prehistorian, Egerton Sykes, was refused permission because of a Russian protest that he had probable British Intelligence connections. American religion-

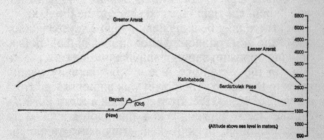

Greater and Lesser Ararat from the south or Turkish side. Although the mountain is within Turkey, exploratory climbing is usually done from the side not visible to the U.S.S.R. Climbing the mountain is difficult: even the different zones have names indicative of the dangers. There is the "zone of swamps," the "zone of serpents," the "zone of wolves," and, finally, the "zone of bears." At any time a rock avalanche can start or the climbers can be isolated by a sudden storm near the summit. As if this were not enough, climbers are also liable to be shot at by suspicious tribesmen.

oriented expeditions of Seventh-day Adventists and the Creation Research Society have experienced increasing difficulty obtaining Turkish government permission to climb the mountain. (There is a growing feeling among church groups that the Russians, who have known where the Ark was since 1916, have dismantled it and carried it off or destroyed it as a troublesome religious relic or reminder.) One of the last expeditions organized by an Italian writer, Mario Zanot, found nothing during their climb, although Zanot contributed the suggestion, enthusiastically received by all the governments in the area, that some of the American expeditions were sponsored by the C.I.A.

The solution to the mystery will perhaps eventually come from the Turkish government itself, as air sightings attract constantly more attention. A 1974 earth resources technology satellite (ERTS), for example showed, in a photograph taken from 450 miles above Mount Ararat an unidentified object on the side of the mountain which, according to the then Chairman of the Senate Space Committee, Senator Frank Moss, was "about the right size and shape to be the Ark."

But there may be a mystery within a mystery since one of the most publicized photographs of the Ark (see drawing opposite) shows a shiplike outline on a mountain "in the vicinity of Ararat," but actually twenty miles to the south. The object was photographed from a height of 10,000 feet from a Turkish aircraft during a routine aerial survey. When the photographs were being examined by a Turkish army cartographer he noticed a clear impression on the terrain of a huge ship—one that had lain there or that was *still* there, under the earth, with an indicated length of 450 feet, fairly close to that of the traditional Ark.

The reaction of scientific opinion, after a preliminary investigation of the site was made by an exploratory party, was that the formation was simply "a freak of nature" and that the erosion of the surface of the volcanic rocks had formed an exact boat shape, with prow, gunwales, and stern—something of a miracle in itself. Further digging into the raised sides of the object, however, has produced fossilized wood in an area and at an altitude where trees do not grow.

It has been suggested by stalwart supporters of the Ark theory that a landslide brought the shape from Ararat although there remains the question of a large object on Ararat that appears to still be there. One remembers that the Ark is said to have descended "on the mountains of Ararat" and that the many survival legends place the Ark or arks in a variety of locations.

But the discovery of more than one survival vessel would strengthen rather than diminish the Flood legend, especially since the vessel which had survived

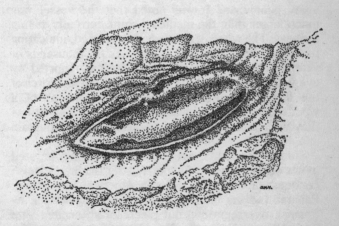

Impression of what appears to be the shape of a ship having a length of 450 feet, like the traditional Ark, found on a mountain 20 miles south of Ararat. Originally discovered by a Turkish aerial survey, this impression has frequently been photographed from the air and has appeared in print as a trace of Noah's Ark or the buried Ark itself. Expeditions which have reached the site report that the shape may be simply a freak of nature although traces of wood in the sides of the formation suggest that a great wooden object may once have lain there or even now be buried in solidified and frozen mud.

would perforce be located in an area of general inaccessibility as well as one propitious to climate or geological preservation.

It appears that other arks, although not recognized as such, may still exist or have existed and been found in various places on and even within the surface of the earth. Harold T. Wilkins (*Secret Cities of Old South America:* 1952), a British explorer and archaeologist, has reported on a few of these "unrecognized" arks that may have been crushed within the folds of the earth during a period of global stress, rising and sinking lands and climatic upheaval. During a tremendous storm at Naples in 1503, according to Giovanni Pontano, a section of a mountain split open revealing the remains of a ship enclosed within the rocks of the mountain. The remains of the ship were observed by many people and it was noted that the vessel was much larger than the medieval ships currently sailing the seas. The wood of the ship was petrified, indicating that it had been enclosed in the rock for thousands of years. At Bern, Switzerland, in 1460 as reported by eye witnesses to Baptista Fulgosa, an Italian writer of the fifteenth century, miners found remains of a wooden ship with masts and a corroded iron anchor as they were enlarging mining tunnels under a mountain at a depth of 100 feet below the surface.

Similar incidents occurred in Spanish operated mines of the New World shortly after the first Spanish conquest of Central and South America. In northern Panama Indians pressed into gold mining service by Spanish overseers dug out pieces of an ancient ship buried deep in the earth. The design of the ship and the massive carvings on the wood were unfamiliar to the Spaniards. Near Callao, in Peru, in 1540, where a search for a silver vein was being made, an exploratory shaft being dug straight down under a hill was interrupted because something was interfering with the digging. When the ground was excavated around the object it was found that the fossilized remains of a large ship lay directly athwart the shaft, underneath the hill.

If these buried ships as well as others half hidden on snow-covered mountains are relics of the Great Flood we may suppose that still others also exist, perhaps awaiting discovery under the sands of deserts, Arctic and Antarctic ice or high mountain glaciers or even, if deep enough to avoid decomposition from teredos and other wood-destroying marine life, at the cold and lightless ocean bottom of the abyssal plains.

Perhaps under the desert in Egypt, considering the Egyptian propensity for burying and preserving their history, an original survival Ark may have been purposely buried, possibly at a point near the Great Pyramid, reputedly built by the "Kings before the Flood."

When doom came to the earth during the time of the civilization that vanished before this one began, some prepared individuals were evidently able to survive the Flood, earthquakes and destruction by fleeing to other parts of the planet. In the case that a new catastrophe, for a variety of causes and interlocking effects that mankind perhaps has not faced before, menaces the present world, what arks can we use for the uncertain future that awaits us?

11

The Arks of
the Future

If an avoidable or unavoidable catastrophe is fated to strike the earth within twenty years as is strongly suggested by past prophecies and present-day computers, one is tempted to wonder whether or not mankind is somehow at fault. If doom arrives will it be in the nature of divine punishment, as an unforeseen result of technological progress, or simply a periodic shifting of the earth's surface over which we have no control?

The variety of reasons for the decimation of the human race available to us in the many accounts of the Great Flood range from specific punishment for man's evil behavior, to an inevitable periodic disaster that was predicted but ignored by most of mankind, and occasionally to combats between the gods themselves wherein man became the inadvertent victim.

The King James version of the Bible expresses the most prevalent concept of the reason in Genesis 6:5

And God saw that the wickedness of man was great in the earth, and that every imagination of the thoughts of his heart was only evil continually.

and 6:11

The earth also was corrupt before God, and the earth was filled with violence.

and 6:13

And God said unto Noah, The end of all flesh is come before me; for the earth is filled with violence through them; and, behold, I will destroy them with the earth.

The inference that mankind is being punished for violence and warfare occurs in many other traditions including the Greek version of the sinking of Atlantis—at that moment engaged in world conquest. Typical among other legends that explain the catastrophe as punishment for sins, are the Babylonian-Assyrian version, wherein the gods are "nauseated by man's wickedness"; the Aztec tradition referring to the gods' displeasure occasioned by "the vices of men"; and the Guarani Indians of Brazil specifying the "ingratitude of men to God and contempt for his laws." One of the most unusual versions is a variant of the Sumerian legend of the Flood: "The gods were displeased with the earth's peoples because they made too much noise." (A decision perhaps open to appreciation by at least a minority of dwellers in today's cities.)

Although most traditions of catastrophe and divine interference to save a selected few seem to be based on man's violent and dissolute character and neglect of observance of divine laws, sometimes among the reasons for destruction we find an unusual and surprisingly perceptive one, almost an anachronism.

There is, for example, the tradition of the Hopi, a small remnant of a very ancient people (the word *Hopi* meaning "peace" curiously resembles the Chinese word for "peace"—*ho-ping*) who have kept intact a vivid record of periodic global catastrophes.

In referring to the destruction of the Third World the legend recounts that a too rapid increase of popula-

tion, the construction of great cities, and air travel
made it difficult (as quoted by Frank Waters in *Book of
the Hopi*, 1969) for men

> to conform to the plan of creation; more and more of
> them became wholly occupied with their own earthly
> plans; . . . man had everything he needed but wanted
> more . . . man kept trading for things he didn't need
> and the more goods they got the more they wanted . . .

At times the reader hardly realizes that he is reading
a record handed down from the dawn of the world as
the Hopi legend continues. In the course of time man
made aircraft, and the cities and countries used them
to attack one another, "so corruption and war came to
the Third World as it had to the others" and, we
remember, the Third World was destroyed.

Along with these apparently modern concepts there
exists other Hopi lore, shared with other tribal peoples
worldwide, which one might label, depending on the
point of view, as superstition or a pertinent philosophi-
cal concept. This is the belief that the earth represents
a living body, similar to the other living bodies which
move upon it and which it nourishes as their mother
through the growing plants and flowing waters on its
surface. The earth lives; its backbone is its axis; it has
vibrating centers which echo the sound of life and
which periodically sound a warning when disaster
threatens the earth and those upon it.

Throughout the world, in the Americas, Africa,
Asia, and the islands of the ocean, it is a belief among
what we consider primitive tribes that the earth is
alive. In ancient Europe and the Mediterranean during
the times of earlier civilizations a similar belief was
also prevalent: for the Greeks earth was a goddess
called Gaia. It was even a custom before drinking wine
to spill a few drops upon the earth for the benefit and
honor of the goddess.

Whether or not the earth really lives in the form that

we usually attribute to life, the concept is an ingenious and poetic one. However, if the earth is effectively alive, it is being considerably harassed by one species of its present inhabitants—the human race. Within the period of the last 150 years mankind has literally attacked the earth. Seen from the eyes of primitive or tribal mankind modern civilization is attempting to kill the earth; piercing, smothering, and destroying its skin, tearing out its veins, smashing its bones, digging out its vital organs, poisoning the air it needs to breathe, and jolting it with tremendous explosive shocks that may break its backbone and destroy its balance.

None of the other dwellers on the earth have ever affected earth to any appreciable extent. They lived on it, enjoying its bounty and forming a life chain that man is now assiduously engaged in destroying at an ever accelerating tempo. Most of the other animals are approaching extinction: 90 percent of all the species that have ever existed have disappeared and the surviving ones are fast nearing the danger level as industrialization and urban expansion destroys what wilderness refuge is left for the surviving wild animals. Even the ancient lure of the hunt has been speeded up so that the large wild animals still surviving are hunted by planes and slaughtered by automatic weapons in Africa, Southeast Asia, and even the Arctic. Within a decade or two wild animals will exist only within habitat zoos, while man will retain only domestic animals and special survivors such as the rat.

The concept of an angry or revengeful earth, previously existing only in the fables of primitive tribes, has lately received a certain consideration by modern scientists and researchers as, for example, *The Quest for Gaia*—Kit Pedler: New York, 1980. Amid accounts of pollution of the earth, sea, and air, exhaustion of resources, slaughter of species, and destruction of the life chain, a more immediate danger has been centralized—that of increasing heat, the waste heat produced in all its forms by modern technology, with this heat itself being considered a terminal pollutant of the earth.

Whether the earth is sentient or not, it may be programmed or committed to its own survival and the effect on the polluters may be the same—a contraction or other reaction of the surface of the earth may constitute within a foreseeable time frame an effectively final answer to its tormentors.

There may therefore be said to exist three possible and fairly close dangers threatening mankind: a protective reaction of the earth—imaginable but unlikely; a cosmic catastrophe brought on by the coming conjunction of the solar planets and their influence on the sun—possible but far from certain; and mankind's self-destruction through use of thermonuclear weapons—which one might classify as fairly possible and perhaps as already begun.

Faced with these potentialities one might well ask the difficult to answer question: *Which way to the Ark?* or the simpler one: *Can I do anything to preserve or save the world and, of course, myself?*

Once, according to tradition, St. Francis of Assisi was asked by a lay brother who was working with him in a field, "If you knew the world was to end in half an hour, what would you do?" St. Francis is said to have replied, "I would keep right on hoeing this field." Fortunately, however, there is still some time at our disposal to stop and perhaps to reverse some of the destruction that has already taken place on our planet which, as seen from the moon by our astronauts in its various shades of blue, seems like the space island paradise it should really be.

There are a few private groups which, aware of the current environmental and social deterioration as well as the possibility of a nuclear Doomsday in the not too distant future, are even now planning an escape route or escape artifact which in earlier times would be referred to as an Ark. These groups should not be confused with individual or collective visionaries who frequently, while waiting to be saved by interstellar spaceships, proclaim their certainty that the world will end on a definite day and month and, when it does not, make new and equally dramatic calculations for the future.

An example of a group action based on an estimate of probable future disaster was recently brought to public attention by a letter to the editor which appeared in *Omni* magazine (June 1979). The letter was signed Tom Gale, of Toronto, Canada, and went as follows:

> I don't mean to be pessimistic but, as far as I can tell, civilization as we know it stands about a one-in-ten chance of surviving past the year 2000. So, while those of us who strive to ensure mankind's survival must by all means continue to do so, it perhaps behooves us to give serious consideration to the only other alternative, should our efforts on this planet prove fruitless: exodus.
>
> It seems unlikely that our governments will be of any assistance, preoccupied as they are with politics, finances, resources, and war. It is up to us.
>
> Project Noah will certainly be vast, most likely expensive, but definitely not impossible. If you have anything to contribute, from practical suggestions, through financial assistance, to your own person as a colonist, I urge you to contact me through this magazine. This appears to be a logical first step.

The reaction to Gale's short letter was surprising. *Omni* received hundreds of inquiries not only expressing interest in the project but many inquiring about obtaining passage on a modern Ark.

The ideas of Gale and his associates do not necessarily imply an immediate series of thermonuclear planetary explosions, although it is considered possible that this will probably follow social convulsions on a planetary basis. His ideas are partially based on some current scientific opinion re the poisoning of earth and its people. On an overview there is the notable increase of radioactivity since 1961. The presence of enough tritium in the world's water to damage the brain functions of future generations, acerbated by the increasing carbon dioxide in the atmosphere, will have an adverse effect on the brain power of mankind, marginally at first and then increasing in tempo until humanity will be unable to operate the complex machinery and processes essential to modern life. This running down of civilization through the products of a technological civilization is but one aspect of the poisoning of the world which may eventually result in the deterioration and destruction of the human race via a general breakdown of society and unrestricted warfare, the beginnings of which seem to be evident to a number of observers.

As a means of carrying out a possible escape plan, Gale and his associates are now engaged in preliminary planning for the designing and building of a privately constructed spaceship which will be built through the use of lately developed techniques and revolutionary new means of drive. It is considered that the new techniques will enable the craft not only to survive the expected catastrophe but to escape the earth itself and, equipped with specialized foods and food plants, technological tools and equipment, and a specially selected group of passengers and crew, colonize a new earth in another part of the cosmos. Such a project, the particulars of which will be, according to Gale, disclosed as it develops, will of course be subject to a certain disbelief, the criticism of the learned, and even public laughter, just as it reputedly happened to Noah.

There may well be a choice of methods to escape from the earth if conditions here become untenable, one fairly obvious one having become increasingly evident in the last thirty-five years—the presence of UFOs in the skies of Earth.

UFOs are explained in a variety of different ways by those who have observed them, now calculated in many millions. To those who do not believe in them they present no problem as they have been officially ascribed to anything from shooting stars to swarms of luminous insects; from planets and the moon seen in daylight whose image is retained on the retina of the eye, to clouds, rockets, searchlights, lightning, and even swamp gas. In addition to the hundreds of explanations given by astronomers, meteorologists, the Air Force, Navy, and Coast Guard, which tend to establish that all UFO sightings are explainable by natural phenomena, and certain behavioral scientists and psychologists believe that UFOs are simply imagined by excitable individuals or populations in today's neurotic world. In other words, if you look hard enough for something in the sky you will assuredly eventually see it or at least believe you see it. (This does not, however, explain the frequent buzzing of airliners by UFOs, their appearance on radar screens, attacks by UFOs on military aircraft and vice versa and, above all, UFO demonstrations en masse over large cities, even capitals such as Washington and Rome, where their maneuvers were clearly observed by hundreds of thousands of people before the security curtain fell on subsequent reporting.)

To those who believe in their actuality it is their purpose and provenance which constitutes the mystery. Many have considered them to be a scouting expedition by aliens preparing to take over the world with its resources and inhabitants; to others, more optimistic, they may be exploratory flights in space *or in time* (our descendants, perhaps?); to still others they are not extraterrestrial nor interdimensional but are the creation of a government or group of governments on earth or even from a secret, nongovernmental earth-wide organization whose purposes remain obscure. To some believers in divine retribution UFOs seem to be an indication of a final winding up of earth's history—a calling to account—a presage of the end of the world.

A striking example of this reaction occurred on March 5, 1979 at about 8:00 P.M. local time over the Canary Islands. A huge UFO in the shape of a cylinder or disk large enough to be seen simultaneously by people on three different islands—Gomera, Grand Canary, and Tenerife—suddenly appeared and remained visible over a period of several minutes, as it coursed through the sky over and between the islands. Pilots of eight different airborne planes in the vicinity who observed the maneuvering unidentified object estimated that it was moving at a speed of over 12,000 miles per hour.

An unusual feature in this UFO report (simply one among thousands occurring in 1979) was the public reaction. As reported by the French astrophysicist, Maurice Chatelain, in a forthcoming book (*Les messagers du cosmos:* 1981), thousands of people in the three affected islands dropped to their knees in prayer as the object hurtled over the land and sea, in the conviction that the end of the world, so long expected, had finally arrived. It is to be noted that, as the activities of UFOs become more frequent and more evident, the belief that they may be connected with the coming judgment or Doomsday for mankind has been strengthened among some segments of the world's population. This reaction takes one back to the fears and hopes once occasioned by the second millennium, which reached their apogee in the month of December 999 A.D.

If UFOs, however, are truly of extraterrestrial origin and not inimical to the dwellers of earth, the idea suggests itself that if they can come here from other parts of the universe, perhaps we can go there, since space travel is not a one-way cosmic path. If we wished or had to travel the enormous distances involved it would be advisable to make contact with those who had already done so, to avail ourselves of their knowledge and thereby undoubtedly change our belief in the inviolability of matter and our traditional ties to the limitations decreed by the speed of light. The most obvious response to the UFO problem is to try to communicate with them for the purpose of opening a way for ourselves out of our present dilemma and to use their help to learn to travel the path through what seems to be the darkness of space but which may lead to a brilliant new dawn for humanity.

Attempts at communication may have already started, although not from our side of the cosmic gap. There appear to be indications, apart from the sudden appearances and dramatic maneuvers by UFOs within our skies, that these alien visitors have left certain messages which, until recently have not been recognized by those to whom they were directed—the inhabitants of Earth. Some observers, mainly among French researchers of UFO phenomena, have noticed certain curious factors in the officially reported landing patterns of UFOs. In other words, the brief landings of UFOs in different parts of France, and presumably in other countries as well, constitute in themselves a mathematical and geometric message which, checked through the most advanced computers, have only a thousand to one chance of being coincidental.

This alleged attempt at communication was first noticed subsequent to a great UFO landing wave in 1954. Certain French astrophysicists and mathematicians found that the seventy-six landing points investigated by the local gendarmerie, if connected by straight lines, made almost 2,000 perfect isosceles triangles and that often the landing points themselves had left burn or imprint areas in clear geometric designs such as five-pointed stars and other figures.

Considering the difficulty of getting individuals of

other planets to understand a message it is evident that mathematics and geometry, existing independently of language and alphabetical or syllabic writing, would be a logical start. Maurice Chatelain, a prominent investigator of the French messages, has pursued this theory to a startling conclusion. Within the angles and inner area measurements of a double hexagon reportedly left by a UFO at Marliens, Côte-d'Or, on May 10, 1967, he has been able, through the use of trigonometry and a computer, to detect that the outer surface gives π^2 in meters and that the surface of the inner hexagon gives $\sqrt{\pi}$ (the square root of π). He has verified this independently of the metric system through measurements, comparisons, and relationship of the angles involved.

One might well ask why, if extraterrestrials wanted to communicate with Earth, they should take the trouble to leave involved mathematical riddles for earth dwellers to unravel, especially since they, the aliens, presumably can hear our radio programs and see our TV emissions.

But the radio programs or signals would not be understandable without a key. Our astronauts, while on the moon, heard "voices" on their headphones speaking in unknown languages, but had no idea where they were coming from. And even if our printed words could be seen they could not be understood by extraterrestrials, just as the "lost" languages of Earth could not be read until a missing key such as the Rosetta Stone could be found.

Moreover, from the point of view of extraterrestrial observers, the greater part of the action on our TV news and entertainment programs would certainly tend to indicate that earth might be a dangerous place to visit without previous communication and security precautions. Therefore, a gradual contact, preferably by mathematical methods, would seem to be indicated since mathematics is without linguistic boundaries and a knowledge of mathematics is a basic requisite for travel in space. Mathematical messages would eventually be recognized by intelligent beings and would pave the way for reciprocal attempts at contact just as the space probe launched by NASA contains as it travels into deep space an etched metal plate presenting, for any space entities intelligent enough to capture it, an earth identification including planetary and atomic information, mathematical formulae, pictures of the earth's regnant fauna (one man and one woman, nude), a diagram of human conception, a selection of various earth sounds and noises, and an encouraging message from then-President Carter.

In assessing attempted extraterrestrial communication with earth, Maurice Chatelain has the advantage

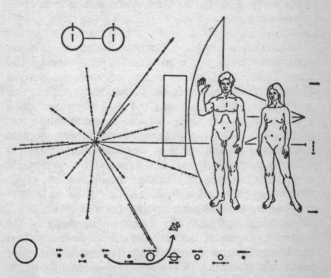

Pioneer 10, launched by NASA and destined to fly past Jupiter and out of the solar system, contained an etched aluminum plaque which could presumably be "read" and understood by cosmic races capable of space flight. The units for time and distance are based on symbols for the two states of the hydrogen atom. Pioneer 10 also carries a variety of earth sounds, including a message from President Carter to the population of the cosmos. (NASA)

of considerable experience in communication through space. During the sixties, over a period of five years, he was Chief of NASA Communications Systems and, prior to that, Chief of Data Processing Systems at the North American Aviation Plant at Downey, California. Chatelain, like a number of other personnel of NASA and other government agencies, no longer bound by security regulations, is definite about the presence of UFOs in space and their activities during the U.S. space shots. According to Chatelain:

> All Apollo and Gemini flights were followed at a distance and sometimes quite closely, by space vehicles of extraterrestrial origin. Every time it occurred the astronauts informed Mission Control who then ordered absolute silence.

In Chatelain's opinion, some of the space travelers may come from our own solar system, specifically from Titan, a planetary moon of Saturn having a physical condition among the planets most comparable to that of Earth. He points out that when our space probe passed over Titan its radio communication was interrupted and its photographic equipment stopped functioning almost as if it were passing through a security zone—but one not imposed by commands emanating from Earth. Perhaps the inhabitants of Titan, if they exist, are unwilling to be visited, at least at present, by the belligerent populations of earth.

We might optimistically imagine that many of the probes from space that are periodically reported on earth are tentative investigations from other planets or planetary systems and are designed eventually to establish fuller contact toward helping Earth and not for purposes of conquest, as the entire history of man's life on Earth might lead us naturally to assume.

Therefore following this communication theory, if aliens were attempting to contact us they might first attempt to do so by furnishing us a mathematical key which the dwellers of earth, if sufficiently advanced, would eventually recognize and to which they would respond. If this means of communication is indirect it has the advantage of preparing Earth's awareness in stages and also ensuring to some degree the safety of entities within the UFOs which have already been the targets of various military aircraft.

The theory of communications through mathematical and astronomical verities is reminiscent of the gradual realization that the measurement and directional aspects of the Great Pyramid of Egypt contain information pertaining to the world and the universe, recognized only when a new civilization reached a level of knowledge approaching that of the old one. The difference between the message of the Pyramid and those of the UFO landing points is that the Pyramid "riddle" refers to a past civilization and is a reminder of catastrophe, while the messages from UFOs, if that is what they are, are an attempt to establish communications with the earth at present and perhaps to convey a warning against the future catastrophe and suggest a way of avoiding it.

What would cosmic visitors be attempting to warn us about that we do not already know? As the most obvious and immediate danger threatening the earth is thermonuclear warfare, it is not surprising that the great UFO visitation began shortly after the development of the A-bomb, beginning in the very areas where the A-bombs were first tested. An interest in the avoidance of the future destruction of the earth would be understandable on the part of other dwellers within the solar system, especially in view of the theory that the asteroid belt between Mars and Jupiter was once a planet, either destroyed by collision or by atomic explosion, the latter event perhaps recorded by inhabitants of other planets with civilizations considerably older than ours.

A further "warning" possibility might concern a comet, asteroid, or something else which, through a vast elliptical orbit of which we on Earth are not yet aware, is heading toward our area of encounter. In any event it would seem advisable, if extraterrestrials are attempting to tell us something, to listen to them—whatever the voices or languages they may be using.

Eventual communication with entities from space could doubtless be accomplished with mathematical codes and computers and eventually by satellite TV beamed to specific areas. As a first step it has been suggested that we relay some of the patterns of mathematical and geometric information which extraterrestrials have allegedly left on earth, perhaps with additional information to show we have understood the tentative messages. Meanwhile it would be advisable for military aircraft in various parts of the world to exercise more discretion in firing at flying objects most frequently identified as UFOs and for command centers to attempt to demonstrate peaceful intentions toward them.

The ever-innovative French have gone one step further and now have an auxiliary landing field near Marliens, lighted by night with a series of blue lights, destined for the use of extraterrestrial visitors only, although no such astronauts have yet landed there.

Although the idea of piloted UFOs and intelligent life in space is usually considered with a certain amount of sardonic humor, it nevertheless remains a possibility and should be considered as an added opportunity for Earth's peoples, through knowledge of its drive and methods, to develop another means of escape from our environment if or when it becomes untenable.

Our legends from an earlier world tell us of a great ship or ships which provided a refuge in far places of the earth, but perhaps after the next catastrophe Earth itself may become inimicable to humanity. Our survival plans should therefore be predicated on an intensified exploration of space; not only to find a refuge but also to expand our observation of the universe, to be able thereby to avoid or control dangers within the cosmos which may even now be drawing closer to Earth.

We of Earth, after a progression of 6,000 years of our current cycle of civilization, are now at a point where we can destroy the Earth and the human race. At the same time we have the concurrent ability to reverse the trend to destruction and to restore Earth to a fairly close approximation of paradise. To do this, however, we will have also to use other Arks of survival apart from ships of the ocean and of space. These other arks of the future are already within our grasp, although at times they are as difficult to find as the remains of Noah's Ark. These present and future arks, however, have the advantage of not having to be built. They have existed for thousands of years inside the collective spirit of mankind, under the incrustations of ages of darkness, tribal and international suspicion and regional antipathy. Their names are familiar—knowledge, reason, cooperation, and compassion. It is evident that the time to uncover and reestablish them is now, while there may still be time to ensure the survival of Earth and *all* its inhabitants.

Acknowledgments

The author wishes to express his appreciation to the persons and organizations listed below who have graciously granted interviews, drawn maps and illustrations, directed him to sources of information, or offered suggestions and criticism in the preparation of this book. Mention in this regard of any individual or organization does not, of course, imply their acceptance or knowledge of or agreement with any of the theories expressed in this book, except those especially attributed to them.

The author wishes to express his especial appreciation to J. Manson Valentine, Ph.D., Curator Honoris of the Museum of Science of Miami and Research Associate of the Bishop Museum of Honolulu, for his drawings, maps, and interviews, as quoted in the text; to Valerie Seary-Berlitz, author and artist, for her contributions to the text; and to Carolyn Blakemore, editor, for her suggestions and editorial direction.

The following names are listed in alphabetical order:

José Maria Bensaúde, President, Navecor Lines, Portugal and the Azores Islands
Lin Berlitz, researcher
Hugh Auchincloss Brown, electrical engineer, author
Brenda Brush, astrologer (PMAFA)
Hugh Lynn Cayce, President, Association for Research and Enlightenment

221

Sergio Cervera, writer, physic researcher

Maurice Chatelain, space scientist, a designer of Apollo spacecraft, former Chief of NASA Apollo Communications and Data Processing systems

Adelaide Cooper, research librarian

Edward J. Czerniuk, Brig. Gen. U.S.A., ret., Specialist in Psychological Warfare

Sara Donnelley, fifth generation descendant of Atlantologist Ignatius P. Donnelley

Julius Egloff, Jr., oceanographer, writer

Hamilton Forman, historian, collector of pre-Columbian antiquities

Rev. Salvador Freixedo, author, lecturer, UFO researcher

Robert Felt, writer

Thomas Gale, journalist

Carlos González, Bible researcher

Professor Charles Hapgood, historian, cartographer, author

Rev. O. S. Hawkins, author, lecturer

India House, Cultural Affairs Office, New York

Ramona Kashe, Chief of Research for Charles Berlitz, Washington, D.C.

John Keel, author, UFO and psychic researcher

Jack Foley Horkheimer, Executive Director, The Space Transit Planetarium, Miami Museum of Science

The Library of Congress, Washington, D.C.

His Eminence, Archbishop Torkom Manoogian: Primate, diocese of the Armenian Church of North America

William L. Moore, author, lecturer

The National Archives and Records Service, Washington, D.C.

The New York Public Library, New York

The New York Society Library, New York

Antonio Pascual F., author, historian, educator

Kenneth G. Peters, Lt. Col. U.S.A., ret., military historian

Herbert Sawinski, explorer and archaeologist

Sabina Sanderson, researcher, writer

Gregor Schwinghammer, airline pilot, former USAF pilot

Egerton Sykes, author, mythologist

S.I.T.U.—Society for the Investigation of the Unexplained

Frank Stably, Lieutenant Commander USNR
Carl Payne Tobey, astrologer, mathematician, author
Maxime B. Vollmer, mythologist, philologist
Robert Warth, research chemist
G. Theon Wright, explorer, author, psychic researcher, Col.
     U.S.A., ret.
Yale University Library, New Haven, Connecticut

Bibliography

Anderson, Wing. *Prophetic Years*. Los Angeles: 1946.

Asimov, Isaac. *A Choice of Catastrophes*. New York: 1979.

Balsiger, Dave, and Sellier, Charles E. *In Search of Noah's Ark*. Los Angeles: 1976.

Baxter, John, and Atkins, Thomas. *The Fire Came By*. New York: 1976.

Berlitz, Charles. *The Mystery of Atlantis*. New York: 1969.

———. *Mysteries from Forgotten Worlds*. New York: 1972.

———. *The Bermuda Triangle*. New York: 1974.

Blumrich, Josef F. *The Spaceships of Ezekiel*. New York: 1974.

Brown, Hugh A. *Cataclysms of the Earth*. New York: 1967.

Carter, Mary Ellen. Editor: Hugh Lynn Cayce. *Cayce on Prophecy*. New York: 1968.

Caso, Alfonso. *La Religión de los Aztecas*. Mexico: 1945.

Chatelain, Maurice. *Le temps et l'espace*. Paris: 1979.

———. *Les messagers du cosmos*. Paris: 1981.

Edgar Cayce Foundation. *Earth Changes*. Virginia Beach, Va.: 1959.

von Daniken, Erich. *Chariots of the Gods: Unsolved Mysteries of the Past*. New York: 1970.

DeNevi, Don. *Earthquakes*. Milbrae, California: 1977.

Diess, Joseph Jay. *Herculaneum*. New York: 1966.

Donnelley, Ignatius. *Atlantis: The Antediluvian World*. New York: 1882.

———. *Ragnarok: The Destruction of Atlantis*. New York: 1883.

Edwards, Frank. *Stranger than Science*. Secaucus, N.J.: 1959.

Edwards, Michael. *The Dark Side of History*. New York: 1977.

Ehrlich, Paul. *The Population Bomb*. New York: 1968.

Engel, Leonard. *Sea*. New York: 1972.

Evans, Christopher, and Wilson, Colin. *Index to Occult Science*. New York: 1977.

Foreman, Henry James. *The Story of Prophecies*. New York: 1936.

Garrison, Webb. *Strange Facts about the Bible*. New York: 1976.

Goodman, Geoffrey. *We are the Earthquake Generation*. New York: 1978.

Gribbin, John, and Plagemann, Stephen. *The Jupiter Effect*. New York: 1974.

Gribbin, John. *Our Changing Planet*. New York: 1977.

Hapgood, Charles. *Maps of the Ancient Sea Kings*. New York: 1966.

———. *The Path of the Pole*. New York: 1970.

———. *Earth's Shifting Crust*. Philadelphia, 1958.

Hitching, Francis. *The Mysterious World: An Atlas of the Unexplained*. London: 1979.

Holzer, Hans. *Predictions*. New York: 1968.

Kennerich, Max. *Prophezeiungen*. Munich: 1924.

LaHaye, Tim, and Morris, John. *The Ark on Ararat*. New York: 1976.

Lamont, André. *Nostradamus Sees All*. Philadelphia: 1942.

LeVert, Liberté. *The Prophecies and Enigmas of Nostradamus*. New Jersey: 1979.

Lissner, Ivar. *Aber Gott War Da*. Switzerland: 1960.

———. *Rätselhafte Kulturen*. Switzerland: 1961.

Miller, G. Tylor, Jr. *Living in the Environment: Concepts, Problems, and Alternatives*. Belmont, California: 1975.

Montgomery, Ruth. *A Gift for Prophecy*. New York: 1965.

Morris, John. *Adventure on Ararat*. San Diego: 1973.

Muck, Otto. *Alles über Atlantis*. Vienna: 1976.

Navarra, Fernand. *J'ai trouvé l'arche de Noë*. Paris: 1956.

Nohl, Joannes. *The Black Death: A Chronicle of the Plague Compiled from Contemporary Sources*. New York: 1961.

Norwood, Christopher. *At Highest Risk*. New York: 1980.

Ossendowski, Ferdinand. *Bestias, Hombres, Dioses*. Madrid: 1964.

Pedler, Kit. *The Quest for Gaia*. New York: 1980.

Priestley, J. B. *Man and Time*. New York: 1964.

Richards, James R. *The Romance of Revolution*. New York: 1924.

————. *The Story of Human Life*. New York: 1924.

Roberts, Henry C. *The Complete Prophecies of Nostradamus*. New York: 1969.

Sendy, Jean. *Les temps messianiques*. Paris: 1979.

Silverberg, Robert. *The World Inside*. New York: 1974.

Sitchin, Zeharia. *The Stairway to Heaven*. New York: 1980.

Sullivan, Walter. *Black Holes*. New York: 1979.

Taylor, John G. *Black Holes*. New York: 1978.

Van Zandt, Eleanor, and Stamman, Roy. *Mysteries of the Lost Lands*. New York: 1978.

Velikovsky, Immanuel. *Earth in Upheaval*. Garden City, New York: 1955.

————. *Worlds in Collision*. Garden City, New York: 1955.

Ward, Charles A. *Oracles of Nostradamus*. New York: 1940.

Warshofsky, Fred. *Doomsday, the Science of Catastrophe*. New York: 1977.

Waters, Frank. *Book of the Hopi*. New York: 1969.

White, John. *Pole Shift!* New York: 1980.

Wilkins, Harold T. *Secret Cities of Old South America*. London: 1952.

Zanot, Mario. *Dopo il Diluvio*. Milan: 1974.

The Bible—King James Version.

The Koran—Translated by E. H. Palmer. London: 1947.

The Mahabharata—Translated by Protap Chandra Roy. Calcutta: 1889.

El Popul Vuh—Spanish Commentary by Emilio Abreu-Gómez. Mexico City: 1945.

Index

About the Author

CHARLES BERLITZ is one of the world's foremost experts on natural mysteries. The grandson of the founder of the famous Berlitz schools, he is fluent in twenty-seven languages and travels around the world investigating unusual natural phenomena and historical puzzles. Mr. Berlitz is an internationally best-selling author whose other books include *Without a Trace, The Bermuda Triangle, Mysteries from Forgotten Worlds* and *The Mystery of Atlantis*.

417